Digital Imagery on Fabric

With all best wishes
Ruth

Ruth Brown

S C Publications

First published in Great Britain in 2010 by

SC Publications
Stone Creek House, Sunk Island
East Yorkshire. HU12 0AP
Tel: 01964 630630
E-mail: info@sc-publications.co.uk

A copy of this publication has been registered with the British Library.

ISBN: 978-0-9554647-1-3

Printed by:
Beltons Print & Media Solutions

Heaton Street

Gainsborough

Lincolnshire

DN21 2ED

Tel: 01427 612291

Web site: www.gwbelton.co.uk

Acknowledgements ...

So many people have helped me along the way that it's difficult to know where to start, but here goes ...

Many thanks to all the people who have generously allowed me to use their photographs to illustrate processes in the book and to those whose beautiful work shows what can be done.

Carol Selwyn-Jones – for proofreading and articulate encouragement. Any remaining mistakes are mine.

Liz and Tony Booth – for being great friends, helping when I got stuck, feeding us deliciously and being splendid guineapigs.

Embroidery Guild – Hull and East Yorkshire Branch members, Rosemary Cousins, Marion Jackson, Norah Lloyd, Margaret Richardson, Alison Larkin, Jill Steel, Barbara Wesselby and Sue Whittaker, for 'rising to the challenge'

Rosemary Cousins – for patiently enlightening my ignorance on all sorts of sewing matters and for asking thought provoking questions.

Craig Burton and Anne Branton– my apologies for having spelled their names wrongly in the first book

Audrey Fletcher - who's always been such a good friend to the family. This book would have been delayed a long time without her help.

Vicky and Brian Taylor, also known as Mum and Dad, for giving me the best start in life anyone could ask for and for telling me "I could do it"

Iain, my husband – the best thing that ever happened to me ....

Contents ...

Image Transfer

Using Digital Negatives & Positives

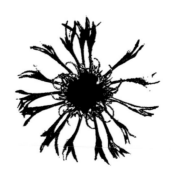

Introduction ...

"... when you have dived off a cliff your only hope is to press for the abolition of gravity."[1]

When I first decided to write this book it did feel a bit like diving off a cliff. I thoroughly enjoyed producing my first book, 'Cyanotypes on Fabric', but had the confidence of ignorance when I started that one. When I started this book I knew exactly how much work was involved, with the added complication of trying to write about such a rapidly changing subject. As I spent 20 years working in IT and now have 14 years experience as a textile artist (some of them concurrently!), I felt unusually placed to write this book, so I decided to jump off the cliff anyway and this is the result.

So, how can a computer help you with your textile projects? Well,

- ➤ you could take a digital photograph and print it on to fabric to incorporate in a quilt
- ➤ you could simplify the same image and create a screen for printing on to a wall hanging
- ➤ you could simplify the same image a different way and transfer it on to aida or calico for embroidery
- ➤ you could create a digital negative from the image and create a cyanotype for a jacket
- ➤ you could use a computer as a design tool allowing you to try out ideas quickly, to combine images in various ways, to take out colour, put colour in, simplify, rotate, repeat, distort, reduce, enlarge ..
- ➤ you could save time by using a computer for some of the more boring parts of the design process, giving you more time for the interesting bits. For instance, scaling up an image takes a second or two on the computer, but can take a LONG time if you are using a grid and the image is complicated
- ➤ Ad (almost) infinitum ...

Apart from some of these specific techniques a computer has another, less obvious use and that is to sometimes give you a different view of things. There is no substitute for drawing something to make you really see it, as opposed to just looking at it. The human eye perceives things subjectively but a computer is ruthlessly objective and will often give you another perspective of an image. Neither view of things is more worthy than the other – they are just different.

So, view your computer as another tool to help you achieve your artistic goals and your printer as just another way of getting designs and colours on to fabric. There is no way I would want to ditch my dye pots, paints, screens and brushes (I LOVE getting messy) but I also really enjoy harnessing the power of my computer and printer alongside the methods I already use. A computer is just a tool waiting for you to use and it's up to you how and when or, indeed, if you use it. The artist still has to make the decisions ...

1   Unseen Academicals, Terry Pratchett

I hope this book is going to be one side of a partnership; I'm not primarily a sewer but, having worked so long in IT, I know my way round a computer and, as a self-taught textile artist, I love fabric. I want to show you some amazing techniques for using digital imagery on fabric – what you do with it after that is entirely up to you. Sew it, embroider it, embellish it, quilt it or just hang it up and admire it as a work of art in itself – a glorious mix of colour, texture, pattern and imagery.

I once had the ultimate compliment – someone told me that I talked about IT in English. I hope that whatever level of IT skill you have, you will find something here to interest and inspire you.

* * * * *

> *If you really want to stop the conversation just tell your fellow textile artists that you are using the 'IPSO model' in your work – this is an old IT term that stands for*
>
> *I-nput (getting your images in)*
>
> *P-rocess (doing something to it)*
>
> *S-torage (self-explanatory) and*
>
> *O-utput (using it in some way)*
>
> *and explains why IT people don't get asked out much …*

There are three main steps to using a digital image.

➤ Firstly you have to get your images into the computer using something like a digital camera or a scanner.

➤ Then you usually manipulate the image, perhaps changing the size, removing the background or changing the colour.

➤ Then you use the image in some way on your fabric.

I've arranged the book in almost reverse order to this, starting with all the techniques for getting your images on to your fabric. This is followed by sections on how to get your images into your computer and how to manipulate them, as these are sections you can just dip in to as you go along. So, let's get started …

WHAT'S A DIGITAL IMAGE?

Well, in simple terms, it's anything visual that can be stored, viewed and manipulated on a computer. So, the most obvious is a photograph taken with a digital camera but it also includes ANYTHING that can be scanned, captured or created in some other way –

POSSIBLE SOURCES OF IMAGES

➤ Digital photographs. These are temporarily stored on a memory card in your camera and are then downloaded to your computer.

➤ Scanned objects – scanning converts things like photographic prints, maps, children's drawings, letters and 3D objects into a digital form. See the chapter on Image Manipulation for a description of what this is and how it works.

➤ Video capture – this allows you to use a single frame of a video as though it was a photograph.

➤ Images from the Internet – just bear in mind that images on web sites are probably low resolution images which will look fine on a computer screen but will not print out well. You also have to consider the issue of copyright. Just because an image is available for viewing to the whole world does NOT mean that it is not protected by copyright. See Appendix II for more information on this.

> Original images created on the computer using drawing software like Corel Painter or Microsoft Paint. You can create original artwork in programs like Photoshop Elements or Paint Shop Pro, but these are primarily for image manipulation rather than image creation.

> Clipart – these are images that are available on the Internet or on CD. They are usually of a simple, somewhat cartoonish nature and are often free of copyright. There are numerous web sites offering free clipart. Just Google 'clipart free' and you'll end up with more than you know what to do with.

WORKING WITH DIGITAL IMAGES

Advantages:

> They are easily stored in a small space – you can get hundreds of images on a DVD or a tiny memory stick.

> They can be copied or printed, any number of times without loss of quality.

> They can be used in a huge variety of ways and can be manipulated on a computer to change, enhance or combine them in more ways than I can imagine.

> The main equipment for using digital images is getting cheaper and cheaper – most home computers will handle digital images with ease and printers are getting better and cheaper all the time. You don't need a darkroom or enlarger for any of the processes in this book.

Disadvantages:

There are, of course, some downsides;

> You are sometimes restricted in the size of your finished image because of the size of your printer. Most home printers only print up to A4 size -11.69" x 8.27" (21cm x 29.7cm) - although size is usually only restricted to width, not length – more of that later. Image transfers let you use your images on larger pieces of work but each image is still restricted to the width of your printer.

> Changes in format or media might make your images inaccessible in the future – anyone old enough to remember betamax videos will know what I'm talking about.

All through the book there are references to instructions in Adobe Photoshop Elements. They are usually given in the form

Image > Resize > Image Size

This means go to the Image Menu at the top of the screen and click on the Resize option and then the Image Size option.

However, my favoured way of working is to use the Palettes wherever possible. See the Introduction to Photoshop Elements at the start of the chapter on Image Manipulation for more information on how this all works.

Opposite: a colour negative of a digital image

Original photograph: Lesley Houghton

Types of Printers ...

In the dim and distant past, in IT terms anyway, most printers used the same mechanisms as typewriters – the impact of a letter supported on a metal spoke striking an inked ribbon - to make letters on the paper. Another type, called a dot matrix printer, used a variable pattern of pins striking the ribbon to produce text and fairly crude images. The height of sophistication for most people was a laser printer but, although these could produce images, the quality was poor and they cost, literally, thousands of pounds. So, there was nothing reasonably priced that could produce images for textile use at home. Things have improved dramatically, particularly in the last 10 years or so. The quality of the print is superb, even in very cheap printers, and the costs have dropped substantially.

Currently there are two main groups of printers that are in common household use. They are split into those that squirt ink on to the print surface to form the image, not unreasonably called inkjet printers, and laser printers that use heat to fuse toner powder onto the paper or fabric

There are other types of printers available such as dye-sublimation and thermal wax printers but these are much less common so I've restricted myself to inkjet and laser printers for this book.

You don't need to know much of the technical side in order to use digital images on fabric but, as with a lot of things, the more you understand the hows and whys of a technique, or a piece of equipment, then the fewer disappointments you will have. You might have artistic disasters but, hopefully, not too many technical ones. You will have more control. So, read as much or as little of the information on the next pages as you wish, but don't miss out the section on 'Types of Ink', as that is important.

Inkjet Printers

These are probably the most common printers currently used - they work by squirting extremely small droplets of ink on to the print surface through a series of nozzles. The dots can be made up of several different colours and are precisely placed to give sharp, detailed images.

Things to consider when buying an inkjet printer

Cost

One of the reasons for buying an inkjet printer is that the print quality is excellent. The other is that they are very cheap to buy – most of the work done in this book was printed on an inkjet printer costing under £40. Of course, you can pay considerably more for a better quality model producing very high quality photographic prints but we are printing on to fabric, which is a broken surface, being woven, rather than a super-smooth photographic paper, so the benefits of having a superb printer are partially lost. However, if you can afford it, a bigger printer, such as one that will print on to A3, gives you more options.

Type of ink

I think virtually every inkjet printer sold today will produce a good print so the critical thing, from a textile point of view, is what type of ink it uses. They come with two types, dye-based and pigment-based. You'll find references to these two types of ink, and what each is good for, throughout the book.

How do you know what type of ink a printer uses before you buy it? There are some giveaways – for instance, Epson badge their printers which use Durabrite pigment inks with a decal on the front which says, helpfully, DURABrite Ultra. Epson UltraChrome inks are also pigment-based and are used in their more expensive printers which typically have 8 or 9 different colour/black cartridges. Their Claria inks are dye-based.

HP Vivera inks come in dye and pigment versions. Also be aware that some printers use both types in the same printer – some Canon printers use pigment inks for the text but dye based inks for images. Lexmark produce pigment-based inkjets and dye-based ones. Of course, all the manufacturer specific information above is subject to rapid change so you'll have to do your own research before you buy anything.

You can ask the manufacturers via their web site or telephone support line, or you can try asking someone from where you are buying your printer. However, although things are improving, my experience is that asking a salesman whether a printer uses dye-based or pigment-based ink usually results in a look of blank incomprehension.

If you want to test the ink in a printer you already have, just print a piece of untreated fabric and let it dry thoroughly – see the chapter on 'Direct Printing' for how to do this. Then wash it - a quick, gentle hand wash will do . If some or a lot of the ink comes off then your ink is dye-based. If it looks pretty much the same then your ink is pigment-based. See the Chapter on Direct Printing for some examples of washed printed cottons.

The cheap cost of inkjet printers is, of course, a mixed blessing. You do get a very cheap printer but the manufacturers will hope to make their profit by your repeated purchase of their inks.

NB The majority of printers are designed to use EITHER pigment OR dye-based ink. You can't normally change the type of ink your printer uses.

Do be careful when you see the results of longevity tests carried out on inkjet inks. A print is a combination of the ink used and the paper with its coating, so the results achieved by, for instance, the well regarded Wilhelm Imaging Research (www.wilhelm-research.com) on inkjet printer inks are very specific to the ink and paper combination tested and should not be extrapolated to fabric. Be very wary of the term " archival" as, again, tests for this are specific to an ink/paper combination so are probably meaningless when applied to textiles.

However, the ink is fairly expensive to buy and can be used up pretty quickly if you are printing a lot of fabric. One thing that can have quite an effect on this is the type of cartridges the ink comes in – some have a combined magenta, cyan and yellow colour cartridge. This means that when, say, the magenta ink runs out you have to replace the whole cartridge even though the cyan and yellow sections may have plenty of ink left in them. My parsimonious heart rebels at this! It is more economical, therefore, to buy a printer with separate cartridges for each colour. The black is almost always a separate cartridge.

Third party inks
On thing that isn't disputed is that third party inks are usually considerably cheaper than own brand inks. Beyond that you will find equal numbers of positive and negative comments on them, depending on who you speak to.

You can often find reviews of manufacturers' and third party inks on the Internet – I found a good one on www.trustedreviews.com. The general consensus of opinion seems to be that in general the third party inks performed very well, producing good quality prints and some had excellent fade-resistance but that the cartridges themselves seemed to have more technical problems than the manufacturers' own inks. Also, own brand cartridges seem to print more pages than third party inks but this, again, varies considerably.

Just be aware that using third party inks may invalidate the warranty on your printer – whether this matters on a £35 printer is up to you.

Bulk inks
If you are planning on printing a LOT of fabric you may want to do some research on whether your proposed printer will take a CIS (continuous ink system). This replaces the original ink cartridges with bigger ink tanks and the tubing to connect it all together. Just Google 'continuous ink system' or 'bulk ink system' and you will find a number of suppliers for these systems and which printers they will fit.

Savings on ink costs of around 70% are quoted but if you don't do a LOT of printing then the ink can degrade before you use it up. General recommendations are to seriously consider a CIS if you are using a set of normal ink cartridges a week.

Do your research before you invest in a CIS. Is it easy to fit? Is it reliable? How much are the inks? Are the inks good quality? Will it invalidate my printer's warranty? Do I do enough printing to warrant getting one?

Size and type of paper
Next, what size of media will the printer take? The cheapest printers will only print up to A4 size (11.69" X 8.27" – 29.7cm x 21cm) but A3 printers, which print double this size, are available for under £200, at the time of writing.

The printer also has to be capable of physically feeding through the fabric plus its backing (see the chapter on 'Direct Printing' for what I mean by this). I usually consider that if the specification says it will print on card then it should feed the fabric through without any problems. Having said that I haven't come across a single inkjet printer yet that won't feed a medium weight cotton on a paper label without any problem. There may, however, be a 'first' at some point ...

Just to emphasise the point about tests being dependent on a particular ink/paper combination, one particular third party ink came top of the group on one type of paper and bottom of the group on a different paper so how can we take anything from the tests when we are printing on a variety of fabrics?

Resolution

There is a whole section on resolution and how printer resolution relates to image resolution in the chapter on Image Manipulation (no, don't switch off, it's not that complicated). So, here, I'm just going to make some comments on how resolution is described in a printer's specification. The maximum resolution that a printer can achieve is given as two numbers. The first number is the number of dots of ink the printer can lay down across the width of the paper. The print head travels down the page stopping at regular intervals to print the next line of dots of ink. The second figure in the specification is the number of times the print head stops to print a line of the image on its way down the length of the paper.

Paper route

Does the paper have an easy route through the printer – this is called the paper train - without any sharp bends?. For printing on fabric, as straight a paper train as possible is an advantage – you will have fewer problems with jams.

Borderless printing

Does the printer you are considering print right to the edge of the fabric, usually called borderless printing?

Troubleshooting

There are two common problems with inkjet printers. The first is banding, where the image has obvious stripes of colour across it, and sometimes strange colour casts over the image. These can both be caused by one or more of the print heads being clogged. Most printers have a utility built in to the printer driver which runs a cleaning routine. For instance, on the Epson printers I have, you simply hold down the button on the top of the printer, with an inkdrop symbol next to it, for three seconds. It makes a noise like the start of a rhythm section for a short while and the printer should then be ready to go. In reality it sometimes takes more than one cycle of cleaning to solve the problem, especially if you haven't used the printer for a while. If you don't have a similar button on your printer then consult your printer's manual to find out how to do this.

Another common problem is that of feathering – this is where the ink is absorbed into the print surface and spreads out to give a fuzzy look to the print. Papers specifically for inkjet printers are usually coated to seal the paper and make a less absorbent surface so that the ink does not feather. For more information on how this affects printing on textiles see the chapter on 'Direct Printing'.

Blockages can be caused by dried ink or by air bubbles in the print head.

Extra Bits

Applications & printer drivers:

Applications and drivers are two different types of software. Applications enable you to do a specific task. For instance, a word processor, like Microsoft Word, lets you write letters or edit text; an image editor, like Adobe Photoshop Elements, lets you change the size or colour of images.

Drivers enable different pieces of hardware, such as computers and printers, to communicate with each other. The printer driver is a piece of software that is installed on your computer to act as the middleman between the applications and the printer.

When you click on 'Print', the computer sends your document to the appropriate printer driver. The driver then converts it into a form the printer can understand and checks that the printer is switched on and ready to receive the document. The printer then produces a physical copy based on the instructions it has been sent.

When you get a new printer it will normally come with a CD that contains the printer's driver that you need to install on your computer. It's normally just a case of inserting the CD into your computer's CD drive and following the instructions on the screen.

There's an old saying that goes – What's the difference between hardware and software? Answer - hardware is anything you can kick! If you've ever worked in IT support then you'll know how often you want to do just that ….

Connecting to your printer

The majority of printers today connect to a computer using a USB cable that links the two physically, or a wireless connection.

Older printers often used a different type of connector called a parallel port, which required a different type of cable to link the computer and printer. The tendency now is for portable computers particularly not to have parallel ports at all so, if you have one of these printers and you are buying a new computer, you may need to buy a USB to parallel converter.

Digital photographs printed on to linen using an inkjet printer and pieced into a small bag.

LASER PRINTERS

Laser printers come in two flavours, mono (black and white) or colour. They both work by fusing toner powder onto the print surface using heat.

What to look for in a laser printer

The cheapest laser printers are more expensive to buy than the cheapest inkjet printers but are durable, reliable and are cheaper to run, in terms of cost per page printed. Do remember that although each toner cartridge will print hundreds of pages, you will need to budget for replacements as they are more expensive than ink cartridges.

Most of the items on a specification for a laser printer don't really matter for textile work – we are usually more interested in whether it will feed fabric and what the end print looks like than how fast it prints, whether it will print on both sides of the paper (duplexing) or how many sheets the paper tray will hold.

> *Should you use re-fillable toner cartridges? Well, it's entirely up to you but while I was working full-time in IT I had a couple which leaked and shed toner throughout the interior of the printer and it was a real headache to clean the printers. I, personally, wouldn't use one but they can be a considerable saving in cost.*

Size and weight of media

The problem comes with a laser printer when you want to print bigger than A4 as A3 laser printers are very expensive. It is possible to buy a small colour laser printer for under £200 but for an A3 version you would currently have to pay nearer £2000

Resolution

Resolution on a laser printer often looks much lower than on an inkjet – those aimed at home/small business typically range from 600dpi (dots per inch) to 1200dpi. For an explanation of this discrepancy see the section on Resolution in the Image Manipulation chapter. In crude terms the higher the resolution the better the image.

Paper route

If you want to use a laser printer for direct printing then look for one which has a smooth paper train – this is the route the paper takes on its way through the printer. Some laser printers have a choice of exits for the printout to come through. One indication is to look on the specification of the printer for the heaviest media it is designed to use. If it will take a medium weight card then it will probably feed your fabric through without too much problem.

I've found that most mono laser printers will feed fabric without much problem but the colour versions are much more likely to cause problems as they often have a convoluted internal path - I have one that has a sharp 'S' bend in the middle and the fabric always get stuck there. Its predecessor had its paper feed and exit in the same places but had a gentle 'L' shape inside and caused no problems at all.

Trouble shooting:

There are a couple of common problems with laser printers. The first and most common one is pale streaks down the length of the page or random areas of pale colour. These usually indicate that the toner is getting low. Take the toner cartridge out and rock it from side to side a few times and replace it in the printer. You should then get quite a few more pages out of the cartridge. If you don't have a replacement cartridge then this is the time to buy one so you have it to hand when the toner finally runs out.

Uneven printing can also be caused by your printer being on an sloping surface. Simply level it off to solve the problem.

PHOTOCOPIERS

A photocopier is a combination of a scanner, to record an image of a document or object, and a printer to reproduce the image on paper or fabric. These two functions are combined in one unit to make a photocopier. Until fairly recently all photocopiers were heat/toner based but many all-in-one printers now have a photocopy facility. These all-in-one units can be based on an ink jet printer or a laser printer. Where a reference is made to using a photocopy for a particular process then I mean a toner based photocopier NOT one of the modern inkjet ones.

ALL-IN-ONE PRINTERS

These are a combination of a scanner, printer and photocopier in one unit. They often include a fax machine and, sometimes, a reader for the memory cards from a camera. They can be based on an inkjet or a laser printer.

You can use these all-in-one printers in several ways. You can use it in the same way as any other printer, sending documents to it from your computer, but you can also photocopy, say, a photograph straight from the scanner on to paper or fabric so you don't necessarily need a computer, although your options are greatly increased if you have one. You can also print directly from your camera's memory card, if your all-in-one has a card reader, again without having to use a computer.

Most have some basic image manipulation facilities built in such as the ability to enlarge or reduce your image or to reverse (mirror) the image ready for image transfers.

Having everything in one unit certainly saves desk space and they are usually cheaper than buying separate units but if, say, the power supply inside the printer fails then you will be without your scanner and your printer rather than just one of them. A small point maybe but it is a consideration.

I'm often asked what printer I would buy if I could have only one. I would find it very hard to pick only one type but I could do most of my current work with a cheap pigment-based inkjet printer and a mono laser printer but I would miss my A3 …. Ah, well, can I have three ?

How does an inkjet printer work?

In an inkjet printer the print head, that contains the nozzles, and the ink cartridges are moved to and fro across the paper by a stepper motor, pausing briefly at precise positions to squirt ink droplets at the paper. At the same time a series of rollers controlled by another stepper motor moves the paper through the printer in precisely controlled steps. The whole thing is coordinated by some electronic circuitry, which also decodes the instructions sent to the printer by the printer driver.

For more details on how inkjet printers work, have a look at the 'Howstuffworks' web site, which also explains the differences between the inkjet technology used by Canon and Hewlett Packard (thermal bubble jet) and the piezoelectric method used by Epson.

How does a laser printer work?

If you've used both lasers and inkjet printers you may have noticed that inkjets start printing almost as soon as you've sent the document to the printer and continue at a leisurely rate, whereas the lasers sit and think for a while then print the whole page quickly. This is because lasers prepare the whole page internally before they start to print (they are sometimes called page printers for this reason).

At the heart of the laser printer is an aluminium drum that has a light-sensitive coating. In preparation for printing the drum is cleaned to remove any traces of the previous page and is then given an even, usually negative, electrostatic charge. The page that is in the printer's memory is then written on to the surface of the drum, as it rotates, using a tiny laser beam. This changes the electrical charge in the areas the laser has covered.

The paper is then fed into the printer at precisely the time when the top of the page on the drum is passing the leading edge of the paper. At the same time, toner is released and is applied evenly to the drum. It is attracted to the areas on the drum with the lower electrical charge, ie the areas where the laser has written the image. The paper with its toner image is then passed round a heated fuser roller. The toner is melted and fused permanently on to the paper.

This is a very simplified version of the laser print process but is enough to give you a good overview.

Direct Printing ...

By direct printing I mean actually feeding the fabric through a printer and printing directly onto the fabric's surface. You can print on a wide variety of fabrics from translucent silk chiffon to silk duppion, from cotton sheeting to calico and from aida to Evolon. You can design and print your own exclusive little gems.

The type of fabric you choose will affect how your image looks when it's printed: a smooth, finely woven fabric will show the most detail whereas textured fabric will break up the outlines of the image, which can be very interesting.

It's a good idea to wash, dry and iron your fabric before you print on to it so that any shrinkage has already happened. Avoid powder detergents as the particles don't always dissolve properly and you could end up with a residue on your fabric that may resist the ink. Don't use fabric conditioner and make sure the fabric is well rinsed.

As I explained in the last chapter, the two main types of printers are inkjets and lasers, so I've split this section into:

➤ direct printing with inkjet printers and
➤ direct printing with laser printers/toner based photocopiers.

DIRECT PRINTING ~ INKJET PRINTERS

There are two types of ink used by inkjet printers, pigment-based ink and dye-based ink. For most purposes this makes little difference but if you want your inkjet printed fabric to be washable then it is important.

If you are a dyer it might be useful to think of pigment-based ink as being akin to fabric paints – the ink coats the surface of the fibre. Dye-based inks need something to help them bind to the fabric, in the same way that a mordant is used in natural dyeing. So if you are using dye-based ink then the fabric needs pre-treating, whereas the fabric for pigment-based ink does not.

If you don't know what type of ink your printer uses then print a sheet of fabric and wash it. If some or all of the colour washes out then it is dye-based ink and the fabric will need pre-treatment - see the facing page for some examples of what you might see. If there is little or no colour change then it is most likely pigment ink and the fabric won't need pre-treatment.

Some fibres are inherently less smooth than others – compare cotton to silk. The rougher fibres scatter the light more randomly than smoother ones so an image printed on them appears slightly duller.

For more information on the differences between these printers and how they work, see the chapter on 'Types of Printers'.

All the pictures opposite were printed with dye-based ink:

1. The original image.

2, 3 and 4. The same image printed on untreated cotton with dye-based ink from three different manufacturers and then washed

5. The same image printed on cotton treated with Bubble Jet Set and then washed.

As you can see, prints with dye-based ink on untreated cotton lose a lot of the image when they're washed, whereas the image on the treated cotton lost virtually no colour.

1

2

4

3

5

Original photograph:
Robert Hewson

In general terms the difference between fabrics printed with dye-based ink and those printed with pigment-based ink is that the dye-based ones tend to wash a little better and are more abrasion resistant because the ink is absorbed into the fibres. Pigment-based ones on the other hand tend to be brighter and more vivid and are certainly more light fast.

It's important to realise that no home printer/ink combination will give a print on fabric that will stand up to frequent heavy washing in the same way that commercially printed fabric will. However, given correct preparation and printer selections the home printed fabric will be hand-washable and will certainly be stable enough to have other wet processes used over the print.

All direct printing is, basically, a five stage process:

1. Pre-treat the fabric, if necessary, so that it's washable after printing.
2. Support the fabric on a backing of some sort so it will feed through the printer without wrinkling or jamming
3. Prepare your image
4. Print using appropriate printer settings
5. Post-treat the printed image, if necessary.

The 'if necessary' comments above will become clear shortly, so, let's have a look at each step in some detail ...

Pre-treat the fabric

So, the first thing to decide is whether your fabric needs pre-treating. If your printer uses pigment ink then you can skip this step and go on to step 2. If your printer uses dye-based ink then you will need to pre-treat the fabric with something like Bubble Jet Set 2000 or Panenka Design's Ink Jet Set.

Several pre-treatments called 'digital grounds' are now available but I'll talk about them later in the chapter.

> *All the comments about inks apply to those available when this book was written. Formulations change and new inks are being developed all the time so details may have changed by the time you read this.*

> *I have read that using something like Bubble Jet Set with pigment inks brightens the resulting print but in my tests I couldn't see the difference so I don't bother.*

Bubble Jet Set/Ink Jet Set

The instructions for using these two products are the same. The only difference is that the Ink Jet Set comes as a concentrate that needs diluting whereas the Bubble Jet Set 2000 comes ready to use. These products are only specified to work with pure silk or cotton according to manufacturers' instructions but I have also used them with linen, bamboo and hemp with good results. However, I haven't done any long term tests with these fibres.

➤ Shake the bottle and pour the liquid into a shallow dish or pan (I use a small cat litter tray).

➤ Soak the fabric in the solution for five minutes then hang up to dry or lay flat on a clean towel. You should be able to treat between 40-50 sheets from a bottle of Bubble Jet Set (32oz/946ml)). Hang the treated fabric up or lay it on a clean towel to dry.

➤ Any remaining solution left in the tray after you've removed the fabric can be poured back into the bottle and re-used.

Although the advice is to use the prepared sheets soon after preparation I haven't found any problems using sheets that have been stored for some time.

NB It's important to realise that the use of Bubble Jet Set is to improve the washability of the fabric NOT its lightfastnesss.

Support the fabric

The first reaction when I tell someone that you can put fabric through a printer is often a blank look, followed by 'Isn't it a bit floppy?' Well, yes, it certainly is, so it needs to be attached to a backing of some sort to temporarily stiffen it. I'm going to describe the simplest, and my favourite, way to do this but will cover a number of other methods later that may be more suitable for certain types of fabric or end uses.

A4 labels

Most people will be familiar with the sheets of labels you can get with up to 65 individual sticky labels on an A4 sheet. Well, you can also get ones that have a single label on an A4 sheet. With these you peel the backing off the label and stick it down on to the back of the fabric, keeping the edge of the label parallel to the grain of the fabric (1). No ironing is necessary. Smooth it down well with your hands, then trim the edges of the fabric.

I prefer to use a non-slip quilting ruler with a rotary cutter to do this (2) - see Appendix I for safety guidelines for using a rotary cutter, they are SHARP. Alternatively, you could use a paper guillotine or rotary paper trimmer, which makes it easy to line everything up and is very quick. However, cheap or well-used guillotines are not always very sharp and may snag the fabric.

The exact width of the sheet isn't critical, as long as it will fit through your printer, but IT IS CRITICAL THAT THE SIDES ARE PARALLEL. The capital letters are justified here; if it is at all skewed it may jam in the printer. You have to remember that domestic printers aren't really designed to take fabric sheets so you need to make it as easy as possible for them.

The only problem some of my students have is removing the fabric from the label after printing. Getting it started is a knack but it may help to leave a small extra margin of fabric on one of the short sides of the panel (3). This gives a bit more to take hold of.

Although the label sheet is A4 size, the actual label is slightly smaller so you may need to allow for this when you are preparing to print. See the section on custom sizes in the chapter on Image Manipulation.

Pre-treated sheets

There are now many makes of ready-prepared fabric sheets available. These come with the fabric already supported on a backing sheet of some sort and pre-treated so they will work with dye-based inks as well as pigment-based inks.

If you decide to use ready-prepared sheets, and they are certainly easy and quick to use and generally give very good image quality, then follow the instructions on the pack regarding drying times and after treatment. I have to say that until recently I hadn't been particularly impressed with ready-prepared sheets - the ink ran badly on some I tried and most used such poor fabrics that they were of limited use. Now, however, there are some really good ones available. Ones I would consider are Crafter's Image by Blumenthal Crafts, EQ Printables by the Electric Quilt Company and Miracle Sheets by C J Jenkins. This does not mean to imply that other brands are inferior - just that I can buy these particular ones in the UK and have been pleased with the results. Just be aware that some of the American brands come in letter size rather than A4 so you may have to adjust your image size slightly and select the letter size setting in the printer dialogue box.

 The range and quality of these ready-prepared sheets are improving all the time and I'm sure others will be available by the time you read this. The two pink/purple flower fabrics in the detail from Lesley Brankin's quilt 'Awakening', shown on the opposite page, show beautifully how digital fabrics can be incorporated with more traditional fabrics to good effect.

However, I think there are three reasons why you would consider preparing your own sheets, the first one being cost. Ready-prepared sheets are quite expensive – a sheet prepared at home will cost around half that of a ready prepared one. There are a number of variables in this calculation, such as where you live, what is available locally and the sort of fabric you use, so it is difficult to be too precise.

The second reason is that you have a free choice of the fabric you use, from a fine chiffon or organza to a light weight canvas. You may be restricted by the thickness of media that your printer is happy to feed through, but that applies to ready prepared and home prepared versions.

Thirdly, if you prepare your own you can take advantage of the user-defined paper setting, sometimes called a custom size or banner setting, which will allow you to print bigger than A4 - you are still restricted to the width your printer is designed for but you can increase the length of the fabric you print. If you are lucky enough to have an A3 printer then you can print up to something like 32.9cm (12.9") x by 112cm (44") or sometimes longer.

* * * * *

Also, be aware that there is another type of pre-treated sheet which is often described as artists' canvas and this is a stiff fabric intended for use by artists to reproduce their work for framing. Because it's the sort of thing I do, I did wash a printed sheet of artists' canvas to see what would happen and, in fact, it was fine – the image was intact. However, the canvas was still very stiff after washing and would have been seriously unpleasant to sew.

Detail of Awakening (63" x 39") by Lesley Brankin

Inspired by the architectural form and planting at Trentham Italian Gardens, Staffordshire. Machine appliquéd and pieced using commercial batiks and fabrics created by printing (inkjet) her own digital photographs onto 'ready to print' fabric sheets. Machine quilted.

Quilt owned by Trentham Leisure Ltd.

If I'm in 'production' mode I found I can prepare 22 sheets ready for printing, using this method, in an hour. I tear strips of the chosen fabric the width of an A4 sheet and stick all the labels on. I then cut them out with a rotary cutter.

Labels can be re-used several times - until they don't stick to the fabric any more. If you keep the backing sheet when you peel the label off you have somewhere to put the label until you want to use it again.

Prepare the image

Check the image size

Next check that your image is the right size to print on your chosen sheet of fabric. To do this go to Image > Resize > Image Size. Here you'll see two boxes. For now ignore the top box which shows the pixel dimensions, and look at the lower box which shows the Document size – this means the size that the document will print. It's made up of two sections, the dimensions and the resolution. Make sure that the 'Constrain Proportions' and 'Resample Image' boxes are both ticked and that the resolution is set to around 150. Enter one of the required sizes into the width or height boxes. The other dimension will change accordingly to keep the proportions of the image correct.

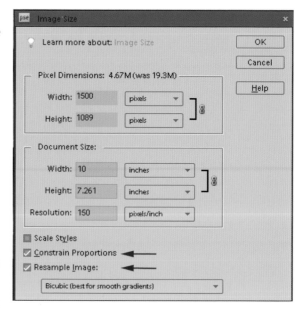

The table below gives the maximum dimensions of the different sizes of paper. Keep in mind that you may get occasional spatter around the edges when you are printing on an inkjet printer so I would recommend that you make your images a little smaller than the maximum dimensions to allow for this.

	Shortest side	Longest side
A4	21.00cm	29.7cm
	8.27"	11.69"
Letter	21.59cm	27.94cm
	8.5"	11.00"

Manipulate the image

This bit is optional. You can do all sorts of things from cropping the image to selecting just part of it, you can rotate the image, distort it with a wide range of filters, remove the background and so on. Details on how to do all this are in the chapter on Image Manipulation.

Check the prepared fabric

Before you feed the sheets through the printer, make sure there are no loose threads or bits of fluff on the surface of the fabric. If you print over these, when they come off there will be a white fleck where the thread or fluff was.

Also, check there are no loose threads round the edges – these can catch in the printer and cause a jam. If there are any, cut them off rather than pulling them!

Print

Load the prepared fabric into the printer

Do make sure you know which side of the paper your printer prints on. On my top feeding Epsons I load them with the fabric side facing me. On my bottom loading mono laser printer I load it fabric side up and on my colour laser I load it fabric side down. You just have to check. On most printers it's better to load one sheet at a time.

Make sure that the guides on either side of the fabric are adjusted correctly. Usually one guide is fixed, the other is moveable. Put one edge of your fabric against the fixed guide and adjust the moveable one so that it is almost touching the other side but not so tight that it grips. The fabric is then guided evenly into the printer.

Send the image to the printer.

If you are new to this then you might feel better testing your settings and image on a piece of paper before you feed a piece of prepared fabric through.

Select the Print option from the File menu which takes you to the Elements print options screen.

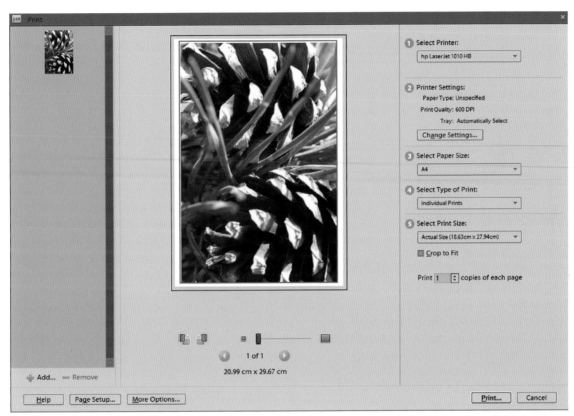

Original photograph: **Lesley Houghton**

Most of the options are self-explanatory:

If you have more than one printer connected to your computer then you select the one you want to print to from the drop-down list in Option 1 - top right above. If you want to manually change the orientation, say from portrait to landscape, then this option is in Page Setup (bottom left). The option to Scale to Fit Media which does just that - changes the size of the image to fit the paper you have selected - is under More Options (bottom left). Those of you using versions 6 or 7 of Elements will find these on the main Print Options screen.

In Option 2 you can change your printer settings - you are offered basic ones first such as selecting the paper size. From this box, click on the Advanced Settings button for more choices.This is where you communicate with the printer's driver and select the settings you want to use - see the next page for an example of a printer dialogue box. Each printer's dialog box is laid out a little differently but they usually contain much the same options.

Firstly, look for Print Quality – this is often given as a list of options such as: Draft or Photo like those shown at the top of the dialogue box on the next page.

As I will repeat at various places in this book, we are printing on to a woven or textured surface when we are printing on fabric so there is no point in printing at a particularly high resolution, as the image

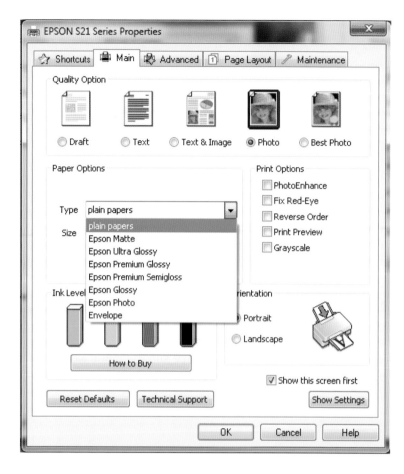

is broken up to some extent by the surface. For instance I can see little or no difference between an image printed on cotton sheeting at Photo or Best Photo. The Photo setting is much quicker to print and uses less ink so this is what I normally use.

Select the Paper Option
This is sometimes called the media type. I have found that the plain paper option almost invariably works well on fabric, so start with this one. Most of the other options, such as Photo Glossy, are designed to work with a coated paper. The colours you end up with are a result of the ink reacting with the coating. You don't normally have this type of coating on your fabric so, selecting the plain paper setting usually gives you the truest colour.

Select the appropriate paper size.
There is a wide range of pre-set sizes such as A4 and Letter but there is also, usually, a custom size or user-defined size which is what you would use if you want to print banners or unusual sizes. There is more on custom sizes later in the chapter.

After printing

Remove the fabric from the label
To pull the fabric off the label, loosen one of the short edges, stick the revealed edge of the label on to a firm surface, like the edge of a table, and use both hands to pull the fabric evenly. If you have trouble starting to loosen the label from the fabric, leave a small margin at one of the short edges when you are cutting it out so you have something to hold.

None of the inkjet prints need ironing to set them. Fabric printed using pigment-based ink just needs to be left to dry thoroughly. Fabric that has been pre-treated with Bubble Jet Set and printed with dye-based inks should be left for at least 30 minutes and then washed. Wash sheets individually in plenty of water with a mild detergent. This part of the process is important as it releases excess ink that might otherwise bleed at a later date. Water without the detergent will not do the same job.

After care
Wash when needed with something like a small amount of Woolite, Stergene, Orvus paste, or Synthrapol, using warm rather than hot water. Pigment-based inks stay on the surface of the fabric fibres, in a similar way to fabric/silk paints, so they are susceptible to abrasion (crocking). For this reason avoid rubbing during the washing process if possible.

As with all textiles, keep your images out of direct sunlight or other sources of UV light. This is particularly important with dye-based inks as they are more prone to fading than images produced with pigment-based inks.

Other supports for Fabric

Freezer paper:
This paper has a waxy surface on one side that, when heated, will temporarily stick to fabric. It comes in a roll, which can be cut to size or in ready-cut sheets. Since this is an American product, just be aware that the cut sheets are letter sized (ie 11" x 8.5") rather than A4 (11.69" x 8.27") – you need to remember this when you are sizing your image and also when you are about to print, so that you select the appropriate paper size from the printer dialogue box.

Using this method, you iron your fabric to get rid of any creases. Lay the freezer paper waxy side up on a firm surface, then cover it with your fabric. Iron firmly with a hot iron on the cotton setting – a cool iron won't melt the waxy surface and the fabric won't stick properly. Start in the centre of your sheet and work towards the edges. Then trim the edges of the fabric to fit the paper. Freezer paper can usually be re-used 2 or 3 times - until it won't stick to the fabric any more.

The main problem I've found with using freezer paper is that, when it cools, it curls towards the fabric and this can cause it to jam in the printer. It can be useful to put something like a heavy book on to your sheet while it cools. This can help keep it flat and it can sometimes help to re-iron the paper/fabric sandwich just before you feed it through the printer if it has curled.

505 spray and paper or transparency film
Labels and freezer paper are probably the best methods of supporting your fabric but if you don't have either and can't wait to play (yep, that's me!) there are other things you can use. I find this is also a particularly good method to use if you are printing on delicate fabrics like organza, chiffon or the lighter weight Lutradur as these can distort as you pull them off a label.

You spray a sheet of normal printer paper or a sheet of transparency film with 505 spray or Spraymount, then smooth a sheet of fabric over the sticky side and trim the edges. The main problem with this method is judging the amount of spray to use – too little and the fabric can catch in the printer, too much and the temporary glue can come through the fabric and stop the ink adhering to the fabric. It helps to let the paper 'sit' for a few minutes after spraying it before smoothing the fabric over - that way the paper is nicely tacky but not wet. Get the amount of spray right and it works very well.

Make sure the leading edge of the fabric is adhered well to the support so it doesn't catch as it is being fed in to the printer. Once it's started then the rest usually follows without any problem.

If you are using transparency film for your support then you will almost certainly have excess ink on your fabric after printing as none of it will be absorbed into the backing. In this case put a sheet of kitchen paper over the printed panel and carefully dab the excess ink off being careful not to rub. There is another reason to use paper – you get two prints for the price of one as the ink goes through the fine fabric on to the paper.

Paper backed fusible webbing

Another method, which works well especially for applique, is to use the type of fusible webbing which comes in a sheet with a paper backing. The one I used was Bondaweb. I find the easiest method is to cut an A4 sheet out of the fusible webbing and put it, paper side down, on a firm surface. Place a piece of your chosen fabric over the fusible webbing, right side up. The glue is thus next to the back of the fabric. Iron on a hot setting (I usually use the cotton setting) until it's stuck to the fabric. Once it's bonded, let it cool then trim the fabric to the size of the paper, making sure the sides are parallel.

Once you've printed on the fabric side, you can cut out part or all of the design, peel off the backing paper and iron your image on to another piece of fabric. Put baking parchment or a pressing cloth over the image as you iron to avoid scorching the ink.

Starch

Another friend suggested starch to stiffen the fabric ready for printing. I applied three thin coats of starch to cotton sheeting, ironing between each coat, and cut A4 sheets out. It fed through the printer without any problems but when I washed a piece of each test a lot of the ink came off with the starch even when printed with pigment-based ink, which is intuitively what you'd expect.

Xyron machine

A lady who came to one of my mini-tutorials on direct printing at a show, suggested using a sheet of paper prepared with a Xyron machine as a support. Xyron machines are used in paper crafts to apply an even coating of adhesive. I tried out the sheet she kindly sent me and it worked very well. I don't have much experience with this method but if you have one of these machines it's well worth trying – just make sure you have the temporary adhesive cartridge fitted, not the permanent one!

Digital Grounds

A digital ground is a liquid you apply to a surface and allow to dry. It then acts as the equivalent of the coating you get on inkjet papers etc so you get good, bright colours and virtually no wicking, even on challenging surfaces.

The two main manufacturers at the moment are Golden and inkAID, both of whom produce a variety of excellent products that can all be used with pigment or dye-based inks. Your choice of precoats will depend on two things, the surface you are going to print on to and whether you want the resulting print to be water resistant.

In a spirit of curiosity I thought I would try backing some fabric with sticky back plastic but first of all it was very tricky to get it to lie flat on the fabric – I tended to get air bubbles between the two. The second problem is that the non-sticky side is very slippy. I found it didn't feed well in my printers and tended to cockle and jam. You certainly would not use it in a laser printer as I'm pretty sure it would melt!

I got a sheet of Perspex cut into A4 sized pieces and use these with a stick-on handle as a template. Since you can see through Perspex it is easy to position the template accurately and you can cut straight round with a rotary cutter without marking it up first. You can, with care, cut several sheets at a time.

This is especially useful for methods like fusible webbing or freezer paper from a roll, where you don't have the guidance of a ready cut sheet.

Golden's Digital Ground Clear (Gloss) and Digital Ground White (Matte) are both designed for porous surfaces like fabric but only the latter is water resistant. The white version is semi-clear when you apply it but turns white when it dries, thus obscuring what is underneath it. This may or may not be what you want.

All the precoats made by inkAID are designed to be used on porous surfaces. I mainly use the White Matte, as it is currently the only water resistant one, but occasionally use the Semi-Gloss. I would prefer to use a clear ground most of the time but as I like to layer different processes together I

Photograph by John Owen

Norton Priory Monk's Head by Jane Thomas

Jane produced this lovely embroidery as part of the Chelford Embroiderers' Guild Summer challenge in 2008 which took Norton Priory as its subject, which she won.

She visited Norton Priory (near Runcorn) and took several photographs of interesting subjects but was captivated by the expression on the face of the sculpture of a monk.

She selected just the head of the monk and then printed it, using a Hewlett Packard PSC 1350, on to linen using freezer paper to support the fabric through the printer. She used the 'Best' setting and 'other inkjet paper' for her media selection.

She embroidered the face with a combination of straight and satin stitch, using stranded Anchor and DMC threads. French knots added texture to his shoulders and hair and his face was padded using polyester quilting wadding to give a 3D effect. Machine embroidered leaves were added to the corners of the work prior to it being framed.

need something which is water resistant so, at the moment, that means the White.

The method of use is basically the same for all the grounds:

➤ Stir the solution before you apply it as the ingredients can separate during storage. Both Golden and inkAID say that their products can be diluted with up to 10% of water. If you are going to print on to a fine surface like silk then this helps.

➤ Brush the solution on to your chosen surface with a foam brush - I've also had good results with a soft varnish brush. I had some problems when I only wanted to coat a section of a fine fabric as the ground contracted when it dried while the uncoated areas didn't. The solution to this is to stretch the fabric tautly on a frame or tape it to a sheet of perspex or glass, brush on the ground and leave it to dry while stretched. Don't brush on too much solution - aim for a nice, even, moderate coating.

➤ Let the surface dry

➤ Print using appropriate printer settings. inkAid suggest using 'semigloss' or 'enhanced matte' paper settings for their semi-gloss product and 'matte paper' or 'canvas' settings for their White Matte. However, I forgot to set this when I did my first tests and got great results with the 'plain paper' setting. As with most things to do with fine tuning your prints, you will have to test the various settings available on your particular printer and see which you like best.

I wouldn't personally use these digital grounds on soft, fluid fabrics as they do affect the 'hand' of the fabrics and stiffen them somewhat. I'm quite happy with the results I get using pigment inks or dye-based inks with Bubble Jet Set - the images are good and the fabrics are still fluid. However, digital grounds really come into their own when you want to print on more unusual fabrics such as Lutradur or hand-made paper and as for printing on plastic, glass or metal ...

Printing on more unusual surfaces.
Soluble Film
This section was inspired by one of my friends who asked whether you could print on the soluble film used by embroiderers. I had to confess that I hadn't a clue! So I tested a few and had very variable results. They are a bit too delicate to use a label to support them through the printer – they tear when you pull them off – but using 505 spray and a sheet of paper or transparency film works well (see the section earlier in this chapter on Supports).

It isn't always easy to get the flimsy film to lie flat on the tacky surface of the paper. I found the best way was to roll your cut piece of film round the inner tube of a roll of kitchen paper then unroll the film gradually over the tacky paper smoothing gently as you go. Once it's roughly in place turn it over and smooth the paper on to the film rather than the other way round. That way the film isn't stretched and distorted as you smooth it. Trim the edges and you are ready to print.

> Both Golden and inkAID have good information on their web sites about their products and what each is good for as well as relevant health and safety information.

> Your tools and surfaces don't need any special cleaners, just water with sometimes a little detergent.

ONE OF THE BEST BITS

Banner Printing

It's a common misconception that A4 printers can print a maximum size of an A4 sheet. In fact, although you are restricted to the width of your printer you can print longer pieces of fabric, sometimes called banners.

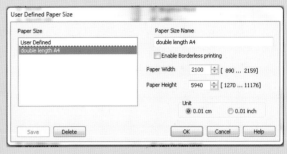

You need to use something called a User Defined Size or sometimes a Custom Size. User Defined Sizes are specific to a printer. So, if you have two printers and you want to set up a non-standard size, you will have to do so separately for each printer. Go to your printer's dialogue box and find the box where you select the size you are going to print to. Usually at the bottom of the drop down list there will be an option for you to setup/select User Defined or Custom Sizes. In the illustration here, I've set up a size which is the same width as an A4 sheet (2100mm) but have doubled the length to (5941 mm). I've given it an appropriate name and have saved it. The numbers next to the paper width and height boxes show the allowable sizes for that particular printer, the paper height being the length of fabric you can print. Different printers may have different maximums.

A long piece of fabric supported on several labels being fed into the printer.

To print a banner, follow this sequence:

Set up a User Defined Size for your printer

Set your image size to the same or smaller dimensions so it will fit on the new paper size. See Re-sizing images in the chapter on Image Manipulation.

Print your image, making sure you select the User Defined Size for your paper size.

If you have an A3 printer you can still use the A4 labels but use two together, making sure that you don't leave a gap between them as this may show up as a line on the printed image. You may also need to support the fabric as it feeds into the printer – if you let it fall over so that the join between the labels opens, then the sticky side of the label may catch inside the printer and cause a jam. As printing banners takes a bit of preparation and quite a lot of ink you might want to try a dummy run on paper using the Draft setting (for speed and minimum quantity of ink)to check that all your sizes and settings are ok and to get some practice at feeding a long item into the printer.

ANOTHER BEST BIT

Tiling

If you want to print an image that is bigger than the A4 your printer can do then you can print the image out in sections that can be pieced back together again later. This is called tiling or sometimes poster printing. In the States this seems to be called posterisation which is a little confusing as in Elements this means simplifying colours.

This function is usually found in the printer dialogue box. For instance for the Epson S21 inkjet printer it is in:

Properties > Page Layout > Multi-page > Poster Printing.

Here you can set the number of tiles you want your image split into, 2 x 2, 3 x 3 etc, each tile being an A4 sheet.

In other printers these settings may be in a slightly different place, such as Finishing, or be

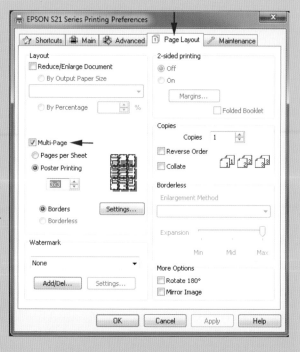

called something slightly different, but have a look round and you'll find them.

There are other ways to tile your images:

If you have an all-in-one printer you may have an option to tile your image in one of the menus. Have a look under the Reduce/Enlarge menu - see your manual for details.

You could also manually cut the image up in Elements then scale up each segment by the same percentage, making sure each piece will fit on an A4 sheet. This will avoid one of the possible problems using an automated method of tiling which is getting joins where you don't want them, perhaps in the middle of a face!

This image shows a digital photograph split into nine segment, each of which is an A4 sheet, ready to be pieced together.

None of the brands I tested worked with dye-based inks. They either wrinkled badly or just stayed wet on the surface and smudged. However, a couple of brands worked very well with pigment-based inks - the Soluble Film Company's gave good results as did Guiletta.

Aida

I've printed on a variety of different weights of Aida and they've all worked well. This lets you print your embroidery design directly on to your Aida ready for sewing. I've included a section on simplifying digital images for embroidery in the chapter on Image Manipulation.

This shows the original photograph of a patch of dandelions.

The main picture is a cropped section of the original that has been posterised to simplify the colours. I've then 'sampled' the colours and printed patches of them, using the marquee selection tool and filled with a selected foreground colour, to make thread matching easier. The whole thing was then printed on to aida ready for embroidering. For details of all these techniques see the chapter on Image Manipulation

Evolon and Lutradur

Evolon is a non-woven polyester/nylon fabric with a soft, suede-like feel. Printing on this is simple. I use 505 spray and paper to support it and print with the usual Plain Paper setting. There is virtually no wicking, but there is a big difference in colour with the type of ink used. Dye-based ink looks dull and the image is indistinct. It is also susceptible to water - a small amount of moisture will move the image around and leave water marks. However, pigment-based ink has good colour and image definition. It is also water resistent, as you'd expect.

Lutradur is a non-woven polyester material - to me it always looks like overlapping cobwebs. It feels like an interfacing material but all the weights, 30g, 70g, 100g and 130g have a see through quality that is very attractive.

I have to say that Lutradur is challenging to print on. The ink wicks badly to give what can only be described as a 'fluffy' print, unless you pre-treat the fabric with something.

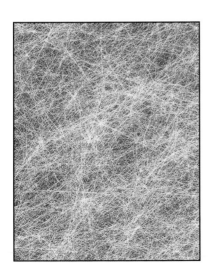

Lutradur 30 scanned over black card to show the structure.

I thought I would try a couple of unconventional products first as I already had them. Dupont's antifusant, which is sold for treating silk so that the dye doesn't run when you are painting, was the first one. I tried this on Lutradur as well as silk and it worked really well. It also survived gentle washing without any problems.I also tried PermaFix which is sold to spray inkjet prints on paper to protect them from UV light. This also worked well in terms of giving a crisp print but the image largely disappeared on washing.

Although the two heavier weights of Lutradur are stiff enough to feed through the printer without a support, quite a bit of ink can go through the gaps in the structure which then spatters inside your printer so I would recommend you use a paper backing of some sort with all the Lutradurs. The adhesion from the A4 labels is too strong - it pulls fibres off the surface when you remove it - but the 505 spray/paper method works very well for the lighter weights. For the heavier weights you could just use masking tape or double sided tape to fix the lutradur to a backing sheet.

This is one of the many surfaces where digital grounds really come into their own. The left hand side was treated with inkAID White Matte Precoat and the right side left uncoated. The results are pretty amazing.

You can't use Bubble Jet Set on Lutradur or Evolon as they are not natural fibre.

There is a 70g version of Lutradur in black. Since inkjet inks are translucent they won't cover a dark fabric so they don't work on the black version. However, if you pretreat it with either of the White digital grounds then you get a lovely, smoky looking image.

Velvet

Some of the best questions come from my students – one asked if you could print on velvet. I tried it and was disappointed as the ink spattered on the pile. However, we found that if you fed the fabric through in the direction of the nap then the results were amazing. It also helps to iron the pile gently, in the direction of the nap, so it lies as flat as possible, before printing so there is less to flick the ink about. The picture of the peacock feather right at the start of the book is printed on velvet and is probably one of my favourite images.

Devore

This was probably the most difficult type of fabric to master. The problem is that the feed mechanism inside the printer, a mixture of rollers and little wheels like pizza cutters, were trying to grab hold of the fabric to feed it through as usual but one wheel was grabbing a thin section and the other one was grabbing a thick bit and the fabric was being skewed round with the uneven pull.

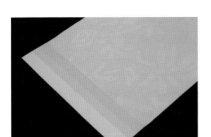

A picture of devore velvet, with its sleeve, ready to be fed into the printer.

I tried various things to solve this problem and finally came up with the idea of putting a paper sleeve on the leading edge of the fabric, held on with masking tape. This gives the feed mechanism something even to pull on and, once the fabric has started to feed, there doesn't seem to be a problem with continuing to feed it through.

Bondaweb

Apart from its use as a support for fabric in direct printing you can also print directly on the paper side and use it as a template or you can print on the glue side ...

Polyester

Until pigment-based inks came along it was impossible to print on to polyester fabrics and have them washable afterwards, as they couldn't be treated with Bubble Jet Set. Now, certainly with Epson DuraBrite Ultra inks, fabrics from polyester satin to polyester sheer are printable without any problems.

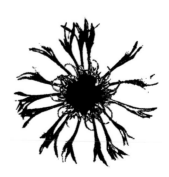

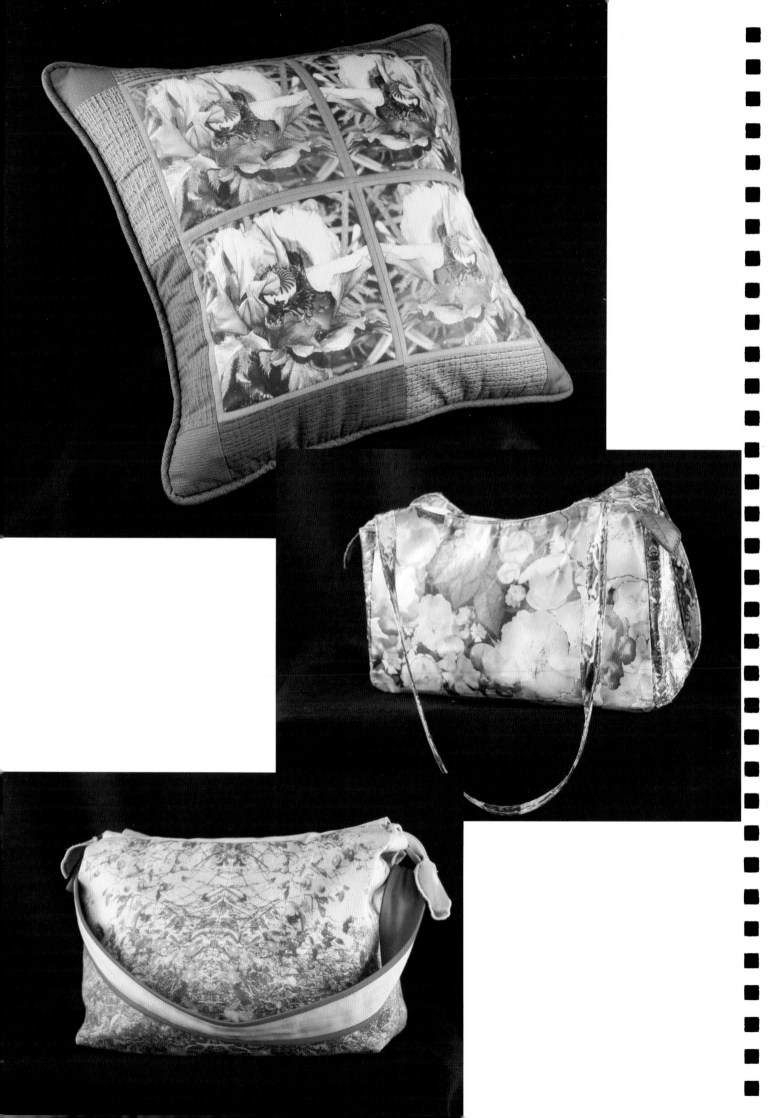

All the fabrics for this cushion were printed on a cheap (under £40) printer using pigment-based ink. The original poppy photograph was cropped and printed on to cotton. The image was then mirrored and printed again. I then converted the image to greyscale and printed it twice more.

I printed the outside fabrics in colours taken from the photograph and the cushion was beautifully sewn by Rosemary F C Cousins.

Original photograph: Anita Yearsley

For this bag Rosemary first created a composite design based on a series of photographs of wild dog roses and apple blossoms. She then made a repeating pattern for the back of the bag based on one of the apple blossoms.

These were printed, using pigment based ink, on to ordinary cotton sheeting. The back, sides and handle were printed in the tiled pattern, with the front using the composite image.

Rosemary used another technique, found on the Internet, for making your own 'oilcloth', whereby the fabric was covered with clear sticky back plastic (referred to as a 'Blue Peter Moment') and then

ironed on a medium setting, using either a pressing cloth or tea towel, until the plastic has lightly melted onto the fabric.

She cropped and enlarged one leaf and printed out 2 pairs (so they would go back to back), added the sticky back plastic, cut them out and stitched them on to make the zip tab.

Original photographs: Rosemary F C Cousins

This second bag in Rosemary's series features a photograph of rose hips that was flipped to create a pair of mirrored images for the front and another pair for the back. These were all printed on to heavy cotton sateen.

The zip tabs were created from pictures of single hips that were again mirrored and printed out twice for each tab.

Original photographs: Rosemary F C Cousins

DIRECT PRINTING - LASER PRINTERS/ PHOTOCOPIERS

I recently found a comment in an otherwise excellent book on direct printing that states that laser printers aren't suitable for fabric. Well I've used them very successfully but they do need a slightly different method of working from inkjet printers.

Preparation

Fabric to go through a laser printer does not need any pre-treatment so the first thing you need to do is fix your fabric to a backing sheet and trim it to size as described earlier in the chapter. If you use labels then make sure they are specifically for laser printers or are marked as multi-purpose (it will say on the packet). Freezer paper is ok to use as well. I wouldn't personally put anything with spray glue (such as Spraymount/505 spray) or fusible webbing through a laser printer.

Print your image

You follow the same procedure as for printing on an inkjet printer. Select the Print option from the File menu. Select the printer and paper size you want to use. On more modern, colour laser printers you may have the option of General or Photo quality. If so, select Photo.

Laser printers often have two paper trains (a paper train is simply the path the paper takes as it goes through the printer). The default train is usually a U shape but they often have another one, that has to be specifically selected, that is shaped more like a soft S shape so the paper exits through the back of the printer. If your printer has a choice of paper trains then pick the straightest one.

As usual, you need to know which side of the paper (or in our case fabric) will be printed on. Load and print your supported fabric one sheet at a time.

Intuitively you would think that an image printed on a laser printer,which uses heat to make the image, would then be fixed on to the fabric, but no. If you wash it at this stage most will come off.

For a description of how laser printers work see the chapter on Types of Printers. The main thing to remember is that laser printers work by fusing toner powder to the fabric using heat so don't try to print anything that melts with heat. I know that sounds pretty obvious but it is very easy to get carried away with the excitement of trying new things and end up with something melted round the insides of your printer – not a good idea!

This image was printed on to cotton. The right-hand side was then washed. As you can see most of the toner has come off

Original photograph: **Iain Brown**

The toner is on the surface of the fabric and needs to be heat set. Place your print, face up, on to a firm surface and cover with a sheet of clean newsprint or baking parchment. Then, using a hot iron, press firmly over the image, trying not to move the covering paper around. Then leave to cool thoroughly. After that it is washable.

This image was printed on to cotton and then heat set. The right-hand side was then washed with virtually no loss of toner.

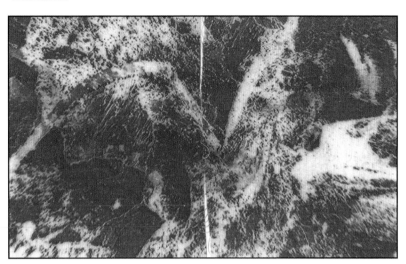

You can, of course, print on to white or coloured fabrics. You could use commercial or hand-dyed fabrics or you could use one of my favourite techniques which is to paint the fabric with silk/fabric paints or diluted artists' acrylic paints, heat set the paint and then print with a mono laser printer. You can see an example of this, using a greyscale version of a picture of some roses printed on a copper and gold background, at the end of the chapter.

This image is a greyscale version of a photograph which was then printed on to terracotta dyed silk using a mono laser printer. Original photograph: **Craig Burton**

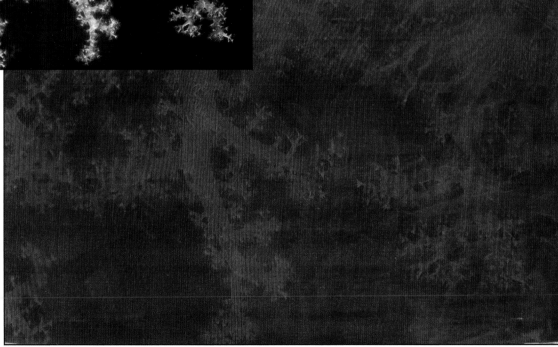

Martha's roses

The greyscale roses were printed on to cotton with a laser printer. The image was heat set and then the flower heads were painted with translucent silk paint which was also then heat set.

Omnicrom foil

This foil is attracted to the toner on a laser printed image. Print your image on to your fabric and then place your fabric, print side up, on a firm surface. Put the foil, coloured side up on to the fabric, top with a sheet of baking parchment and iron with a medium hot iron. The foil is transferred only to the toner covered areas of the fabric, ie the image. The foil transfer isn't as uniform on fabric as it seems to be on paper but I prefer the variegated result to uniform bling.

Martha's roses 2

This is a variation on the red roses opposite. I painted the background with metallic gold and copper textile paints. This was dried and heat set then mounted on an A4 label for support. The greyscale roses were then printed on with a laser printer.

Image Transfer ...

Image transfer typically involves printing an image on a substrate such as a piece of transparency film or a sheet of paper and then transferring the image from this intermediate medium on to the fabric.

Unlike direct printing, image transfer doesn't require the fabric itself to be passed through a printer, so transferred images can be added easily to larger pieces of work. Most transfers can be overlapped to give a collaged effect and there are also techniques you can use after you have made your prints but before you transfer the image to your fabric. These are mentioned in the relevant sections.

Obviously directly printed panels can be appliquéd on to a larger piece of fabric or used as part of a pieced item but here I'm talking about adding images to a large piece of fabric without sewing.

You can also, of course, transfer images on to coloured fabric but bear in mind that neither inkjet nor laser printers have white ink/toner so any white or very pale areas of your images will end up the colour of the underlying fabric – could be interesting?

There are a few things to consider before you start transferring images:

➤ Most of the techniques in this section need the image to be reversed ie mirrored before it's printed if the image is to be the right way round when it's on the fabric, something that is only really important if text is involved and you want to be able to read it - Image > Rotate > Flip Horizontal.

Processes like mirroring images are described in more detail in the chapter on Image Manipulation.

Original image

The same image, mirrored, then printed on to transparency film or paper

Image transferred on to a loose weave linen, using textile medium - see later in the chapter for how to do this.

➤ Consider if copyright rules allow you to use that particular image for the purpose you have in mind (see Appendix II). Of course, if the photogragh or artwork is your own, you'll have no problems here.

➤ Some of these transfer techniques work better, or only, with certain types of printer. For instance, medium transfers only work with inkjet printers and solvent transfers only work with laser printers. I'll tell you at the beginning of the description of each technique which type of printer is needed.

➤ make sure the fabric you are going to use is clean, smooth and dry if you want a crisp, clean transfer.

I'm going to describe three main types of techniques for transferring images on to fabric; using transfer paper, using solvents and using textile medium.

Transfer paper

I was deterred from using transfer paper, sometimes called T-shirt transfer paper, for a long time because of the nasty, rubbery feel of the end result. However, some of the modern versions are really very good, if used properly and applied to an appropriate fabric. Even the best transfer papers, if used on, say, a fine silk, will give an unpleasant plasticy feel but if used on something like linen, where the texture of the fabric can come through the transfer then the result can be great.

Media like transfer paper are forever changing and developing so please take the following as guidelines only – always read the instructions on the pack. The majority follow the same method but there are occasional differences. Check on the packet to see if there are any restrictions regarding the fibres that brand of transfer paper is suitable for.

Inkjet transfers for white or light coloured fabrics

I'm going to start with the most common type of transfer paper, the one that is designed for use with inkjet printers for transfer on to white or light coloured fabric. The general process is:

1. Prepare your image so it's the right size to fit on your transfer paper - Image > Resize > Image Size.
2. Print it on to a sheet of transfer paper.
3. Place it face down on the fabric and iron it, with a hot iron, on to your fabric.
4. Pull off the transfer paper

➤ Make sure you print your image on the correct side of the paper – they usually have one plain side and one with a printed grid or pattern. You print on the plain side and iron on the patterned side. Most cheap home printers don't have a media setting for transfer paper but the plain paper setting in the printer dialogue box is usually fine. See the chapter on Direct Printing if you aren't sure how to set this.

➤ Allow the print to dry thoroughly before the image is transferred. Recommendations vary between 5 and 30 minutes. I use the longer period for all of them.

➤ Pre-heat your iron to the hottest setting your fabric will take (usually cotton/linen) before starting the transfer. Don't worry about using a hot iron on silk – it's much tougher than most people think.

➤ Use a hard surface, covered with something like a folded sheet, rather than an ironing board, which is usually too soft.

➤ Iron the printed fabric before starting the transfer to warm it up, then place the transfer paper over the fabric, image side down.

➤ Iron all over to lightly stick the transfer in place then iron each area for a good couple of minutes with pressure. Not enough heat is probably the most common cause of transfers failing. Some makes specify a longer period of ironing - just follow the instructions for your chosen brand.

➤ Make sure the transfer is hot all over before trying to pull the paper backing off.

➤ Pull the backing off in one smooth movement along the length of the fabric, rather than from the corner, to avoid distortion. (the instructions vary with the make – some say to pull off while hot, some say to leave to cool before removal.

➤ Turn the fabric image side up, cover with baking parchment and iron with pressure. This warms the image up again and drives it into the fibres of the fabric, improving the look and reducing the plasticy feel. This bit isn't usually in the manufacturer's instructions but it does improve the end result for most.

➤ Washing instructions usually say wash gently,

I decided to do a fairly extreme washing test with my samples. One set I washed carefully by hand and line dried them. A second set I washed in the washing machine with normal detergent. I then tumble dried them on the lower setting. All the makes and types I tested survived the extreme test and some did remarkably well. Those that did wrinkle during washing could be recovered by steam ironing on the back until they were smooth again.

I wouldn't recommend this as a general practice though.

The Ivy leaves were cut out from the original photograph (above) in Photoshop Elements and transferred on to linen using transfer paper for white or light-coloured fabric. You can see how the weave of the linen shows through and enhances the look of the transfer.

End Game (30" x 30") by Lesley Brankin

A painted wholecloth inspired by Lesley's son's love of chess. The fabric was printed and painted using artists' acrylics and silk paints. The chessmen were created by loading a digital image into a photo manipulation program and applying edge detection techniques, which create the effect of a coloured line drawing. These were then printed onto T-shirt transfer paper, cut out and ironed into place. The black pieces are a digital negative of the white.

Machine quilted with embroidered highlights.

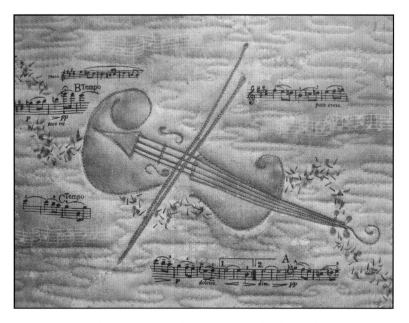

Violin (12" x 9")

by Lesley Brankin

This quilt was inspired by Elgar's Violin Concerto. The instrument's outline was monoprinted using a gutta pen and the design, when dry, was flooded with dilute silk paints. The musical notation was created in two ways: firstly, using a commercial card 'peel off' as a resist (pale notes) and secondly, computer printing sheet music* onto t-shirt transfer paper (dark notes). Machine quilted with feature hand embroidery and beading.

* from Elgar's Salut D'Amour courtesy of freescores.com

don't use bleach, don't dry clean and don't tumble dry. Use a piece of baking parchment over the image if you need to iron it. I usually just iron it on the back if it's crinkled in the wash.

Notes:

➤ One thing I've found during my tests is that pigment based inks used with some of the transfer papers result in a slightly strange greenish colour cast after being ironed on to the fabric. None of the papers I tried had this colour cast when used with dye based inks. I don't know whether this will apply to all pigment inks but it's something to be aware of.

➤ The transfer looks and feels better after it's been washed.

➤ If you transfer to coloured fabric with these papers the colour will show through. This can work very well with mono images eg tea stained fabric with a mono print gives an 'aged' look.

➤ If your image doesn't cover all the transfer sheet then cut off the excess paper leaving a small margin round the image. For the ivy transfer on the previous page, I cut the spare paper from round the edges and from between the individual leaves to reduce the plastic feel of the end result to a minimum.

➤ If you pin through the transfer and the pin marks show, then simply put a piece of baking parchment over the transfer and re-iron it. The holes normally then soften and close up.

Ideas for using transfer paper

You might like to consider some of the following suggestions for slightly more unusual uses for transfer paper.

➤ Try cutting the transfer up before applying to fabric eg stripes, cubes, or a kaleidoscope pattern.

➤ Draw on the fabric with, for instance, watercolour crayons and then iron unprinted transfer paper over your design to fix it to the fabric. This is one way to make a permanent image from a medium that is not designed to be permanent on fabric.

I hesitate to recommend specific makes as they are changing rapidly and, to be honest, most will do a reasonable job. However there are a couple that I'd like to mention.

Firstly, JetFX has one main advantage over the rest currently available, and that is that it remains flexible after the transfer. so it works better on stretchy fabrics. Follow the instructions on the pack which include pulling the transfer gently in all directions while the decal is still warm. This helps the transfer bed down into the fabric.

The other one is called Decadry, available from Staples - I'm picking this one out because it is cheaper than most but gives a transfer that is as good or better than more expensive brands. It also has a nice touch in that the printing on the back of the paper changes colour when it is hot enough so you don't have to guess if it has been ironed enough.

(Two days before this book went to the printers I noticed that the latest pack of Decadry didn't have the heat sensitive printing on the papers any more - what a shame!)

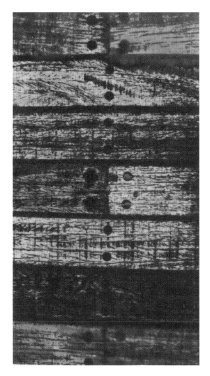

For this test piece I printed a photograph of an old wooden pier floor on to a sheet of JetFX. I then coloured each section with a different medium. I used ordinary coloured pencils, watercolour pencils, watercolour paints, wax crayons, silk paints, pastels and charcoal.

I let everything dry thoroughly and then transferred the image on to some cotton. The only problem I had was I found I had used the wax crayon too heavily and it oozed out the side when it was ironed. On another piece I used it more sparingly and it was fine.

It's a good idea to put something under the recipient fabric as some of the colour of the image can come through.

➤ Print a greyscale or black and white image on to transfer paper and then colour the image using, for instance, watercolour paints, pastels, wax crayons, watercolour crayons etc. If you use any wet media then only use it sparingly and make sure it is thoroughly dry before you do the transfer. If you use any waxy media then don't take them right up to the edges of your image as they may melt and flow when heated by the iron.

➤ If you want to 'distress' your image then one option is to gently sandpaper the edges of the print and any other areas you want scuffing, with the emphasis on 'gently'. Alternatively you could scratch into it with a needle, or a paperclip - if you'd like to scratch lettering into your print then remember that it needs to be reversed so that it reads correctly when it's transferred on to the fabric.

➤ Another way to modify the image after printing, if you've used dye-based ink is to use water to move the ink around. You can use a brush moistened with water or even gently dribble water down the image. Again, make sure the paper is thoroughly dry before you do the transfer.

➤ If you want to use a piece of inkjet printed fabric for something that could get scuffed, like a handbag, then you could iron a piece of transfer paper over the printed image to make it more resistent to abrasion.

Inkjet transfers for dark coloured fabrics

Transfer papers designed for use on dark fabrics, such as Lazertran Textile Dark or jetFX dark, generally use a slightly different method. Note that these transfer papers give an opaque panel on the fabric so its original colour doesn't show through. If you use a transfer paper for white or pale fabric on dark fabric it just visually disappears.

Notes:

➤ The image needs to be printed the right way round, NOT a mirror image.

➤ Peel the paper coating off and place the membrane with the printed image, on to the fabric, image side up. Pull the paper off in one smooth pull if possible as the image may crease if you stop part way through the pull.

➤ Place a sheet of baking parchment over the image and iron.

These papers for dark fabrics give a much stiffer feel to the fabric and, I think, are only suitable for heavier weight fabric. However, the available papers are changing all the time so, watch this space.

Again, the jetFX product is worthy of mention as it gives the least stiffness of those I've tried. For the sample on the left I inverted the ivy image used earlier in the chapter to give blues and purples. I changed the colour of the background to black so it would blend in with the black linen and transferred the image using the instructions on the pack.

Laser transfers on silk

Although most transfer papers will work on silk, the slightly plasticy feel of the image is accentuated on silk and, for me, just doesn't enhance the fabric.

There is at least one product specifically designed to work on silk and this is Lazertran Silk. This is designed for use with a laser printer **ONLY** and has a different method again.

➤ Print the mirrored image on to the shiny side of a sheet of Lazertran Silk.

➤ Place it, image side up on to a firm surface.

➤ Lay the silk on top of the image, right side facing the image, and iron firmly with a hot iron to stick the silk to the image. Too little ironing or not enough heat can result in a poor transfer.

➤ Lift carefully and place, paper side down, in a tray of clean, warm water until the paper floats off

➤ Lift the silk out and place, image side down, on an old sheet.

➤ Gently iron the back of the silk until it is dry.

➤ Turn the fabric over and put a piece of baking parchment over the image and iron with a hot iron to drive the image into the fibres of the fabric. When everything is cool again remove the baking parchment

If you don't have a laser printer then you can take your image to your local copy shop and ask them if they will photocopy it on to your transfer paper for you.

These transfers are beautifully delicate but are not as robust as the inkjet ones. However, they will withstand very gentle washing.

Solvent transfer

This method is used to transfer toner based prints ie from laser printers or toner based photocopiers on to your fabric and gives a lovely, subtle, slightly distressed image which I really like.

A number of different solvents can be used ranging from Citra Solv to Xylene, all with differing amounts of risk. I use either Citra Solv, which is sold as a concentrated cleaning product, or

This picture of my Great Aunt Dora was transferred on to tea stained silk crepe satin using Lazertran Silk. The hand of the silk was still beautifully soft.

acetone, which is used for nail varnish remover but even these should be used with caution.

PLEASE READ THE HEALTH AND SAFETY RECOMMENDATIONS IN APPENDIX 1

Prepare your image

As with all these techniques, the first thing is to prepare your image by doing any manipulations you want to do and re-sizing it to suit the size of paper you are going to print on. For this technique you also need to mirror your image if you want it to be the right way round on the fabric.

Print the image

Now print your image on to paper. Use a sheet of thin paper – 80g cartridge (typing) paper is fine. Use the cheapest, thinnest paper you can find for this – it will take less solvent to achieve the transfer.

Do the transfer

➤ I prefer to fix the fabric to a support so it doesn't move around. I tape it to a sheet of perspex or glass with masking tape.

➤ Put your print face down on the fabric with a strip of tape at one of the short edges to form a hinge

➤ Wearing gloves, moisten a ball of cotton wool or kitchen roll with your chosen solvent and then put the lid back on the bottle.

➤ Use your pad with solvent to moisten the back of the copy. The emphasis here is moisten, not soak. Use only enough so that the paper turns translucent.

➤ Keeping the paper still with your other hand, continue rubbing the back firmly with the pad. The toner is softened by the solvent and the image then transfers to the fabric. You can check the progress of the transfer by lifting a corner of the paper and peeking underneath.

➤ When all the image is transferred, remove the paper and leave the fabric to dry thoroughly in a well ventilated area until all the smell has gone.

➤ If the image smears then you are using too much solvent or you have moved the paper while you were rubbing the back. The general guideline is to use the minimum of solvent and good pressure.

The image is then washable.

Notes:

➤ Images printed on old mono laser printers are probably the easiest to transfer. Modern mono laser prints and, particularly, colour laser prints can be a problem. I find for colour prints it helps if you moisten the fabric with the solvent before you start the transfer, and smooth the print

Put the lid straight back on after moistening your kitchen paper - it won't then evaporate and it won't matter if someone knocks it over! Citra Solv bottles are particularly top heavy.

I learnt this the hard way when a student knocked over a bottle of Citra Solv in a workshop and we had to vacate the room for several hours as the smell was so strong

Nitrile gloves tend to be more solvent resistant than latex ones.

Apply the solvent sparingly, keeping the paper and fabric still. Note the fetching blue gloves.

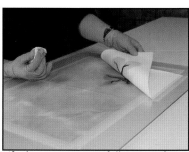
Life the paper up carefully to see if the transfer is done.

George the gecko, back on a wall!

Challenge

A while ago I joined my local branch of the Embroiderers' Guild in the hope that I would finally learn how to sew! Rather cheekily, being a newcomer, I set them a challenge, which was taken up with enthusiasm. I wanted to see what people who really could sew would do with one of the techniques from the book and I picked solvent transfer.

I prepared three images for the challenge. The first was a spray of leaves; I removed the background and simplified the image – see the chapter on Image Manipulation for suggestions on how to do this. The second was a simple mesh of lines that I drew on paper, then scanned to make a digital image. The third was based on a silk painting I did many years ago. I photographed the painting, converted it to greyscale and used the threshold filter in Elements to simplify it. All three images were printed using a Hewlett Packard Laserjet 1100 mono laser printer on to thin paper and then transferred on to fabric with Citra Solv.

I gave the group the choice of these three images on a fine cotton or on silk crepe satin. Of the eight who took up the challenge, five picked the spray of leaves, two picked the mesh of lines and one chose the lilies. All except two chose to work on cotton.

The results, as you can see, were excellent!

The Hull and East Riding Branch of the Embroiderers' Guild was formed in 2000 and is made up of friendly, welcoming, knowledgeable people who share a love of all things to do with stitch. They meet up once a month to listen to speakers, participate in practical sessions, share ideas, solve problems and tell jokes! For contact information look on the Embroiderers' web site:

www.embroiderersguild.com

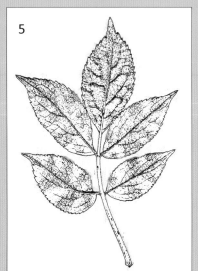

Alison Larkin - "Seasons", based on leaves through the seasons, using split silk threads and satin, stem and straight stitches.

1. *Rosemary Cousins - Rosemary has created a shadow effect made by an upper layer of chiffon stitched with varigated yellow/brown silk thread in running stitch. The lower layer (printed) utilises green silk thread in running stitch.*

2. *Sue Whittaker - Sue used single ply Appleton's Medici wools and a variety of stitches for her version of the leaves.*

3. *Barbara Wesselby - the addition of gold work, gold kid and gold beads give a regal look to Barbara's work.*

4. *Marion Jackson - Marion took the basic design and added a lovely spray of beaded flowers.*

5. *Original image*

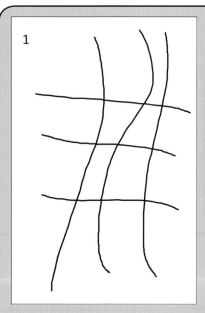

1 - mesh, original

2. Margaret Richardson - a sampler using a lovely mix of stitches, knots and embellishments.

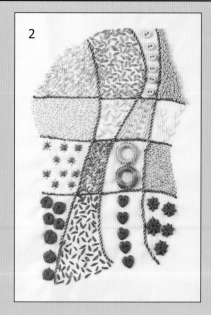

3. Norah Lloyd - a witty interpretation of the original image using a painted background and stitched birds.

4. Lilies, original

5. Jill Steel - detail of a delicate painted and quilted version of the design.

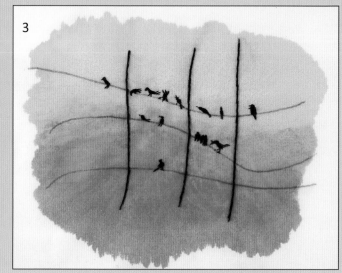

down. Then moisten the back of the print with a little solvent and leave them in contact with each other for a short while before you start the transfer. Then take your time using more pressure. Some laser prints with a heavy, plastic feel may not transfer well at all. If Citra Solv isn't working for a particular print then try acetone, taking suitable precautions of course.

After you have your image transferred and everything is dry then you can draw or paint over the image using translucent silk or fabric paints, if you want the image to show through, or opaque paints to obscure part of the design. You could also use fabric crayons or markers etc.

TEXTILE MEDIUM TRANSFER

In terms of the processes used, this works in a similar way to a solvent transfer but it uses an inkjet printer with transparency film rather than a laser printer and paper. The image is printed on to the film and is then pulled off the film and fixed on to the fabric with an acrylic medium. You often get a deliciously distressed look, like old photographs.

Acrylic medium is a fluid that forms the base for acrylic paints. Think of it as fabric paint without the pigment. If you use a medium specifically designed for textile use called, not surprisingly, textile medium, then this has the minimum effect on the hand of the fabric.

You can use a wide range of surfaces for this process - the acrylic medium will bond to virtually anything, natural fibre fabrics, synthetics, commercial or hand-dyed or hand-painted fabrics or non-woven synthetic fabrics such as Lutradur or Evolon.

Prepare your image

As with all these techniques, the first thing is to prepare your image by doing any manipulations you want to do and by re-sizing it to suit the size of transparency film you are going to print on. For this technique you also need to mirror your image if you want it to be the right way round on the fabric.

Print the image

Now print your image on to the film using the plain paper setting in the printer dialogue box. Many printers have a specific media option for transparencies but, for this purpose I prefer to use the Plain Paper setting as it deposits more ink on to the transparency and, I think, gives a better transfer. You may need to test your printer to see which one gives you the best result.

Of the printer inks I've tried I think the pigment inks give the best results for this method. Dye based inks do work but tend to smudge very easily.

Make sure the transparency film is suitable for your type of printer ie inkjet transparencies for an inkjet printer and laser transparencies for a laser printer. Inkjet film is smooth on one side and rough on the other – you print on the rough side.

If you inadvertently use laser transparency film you won't damage your printer but the ink will usually smear or run because it is smooth . Also be aware that HP inkjet printers usually need a visible leading edge in order to know when to start printing – they can't detect the leading edge of a transparency, so film sold specifically for HP printers has a thin white strip along one of the short edges. This is the end you feed in first.

Some Epson printers won't feed transparency film at all, even with a leading strip. The only way I've found is to tape the film to a sheet of white paper on the leading edge. The film will then feed properly. If you are buying a new printer then look at the part of the specification that deals with media types and make sure transparency film is specified.

It doesn't seem to make much difference what brand of transparency film you buy. I just get the cheap version from my local office supplies shop. However, there is another type available that is sold specifically for making photographic negatives. It is coated with fine ceramic particles that abosrb the ink extremely well. These are excellent for making digital negatives which are covered later in the book but they are useless for image transfer as they just will not let the ink go.

Transfer to fabric

➤ Use masking tape on all four sides to fasten your chosen fabric to a support, eg a sheet of Perspex or glass, so it doesn't move around. Alternatively, put a sheet of freezer paper under the fabric and tape both on to a working surface or table.

➤ Next dilute the textile medium with an equal amount of water. A higher proportion of water to medium tends to reduce the slightly plastic feel of the end result but too much water can result in a poor transfer or one that won't stand up well to washing.

➤ Moisten the fabric with the diluted textile medium making sure to paint up to the edge of the image. The key word here is 'moisten' – you want the minimum amount of medium to effect the transfer. You may need to do a couple of tests as a number of things affect the amount of medium you need such as the fibre, weave and thickness of the fabric you are using and the make and type of medium you are using.

➤ Place the transparency printed side down on the damp fabric and tape one edge to form a hinge so that you can lift it to check on the progress of the transfer without it moving around.

➤ Smooth the transparency down over the moist fabric from the taped hinge down to the bottom to smooth out any trapped air bubbles.

➤ Burnish the back of the transparency with a brayer (small hard roller) using firm smooth strokes in one direction only (top to bottom) until the image has transferred to the fabric. You can lift the corner of the transparency to see how much of the image has transferred. Don't expect all the ink on the transparency to transfer to the fabric – there is often a ghost image left. You can alternatively use the back of a spoon in small, circular movements to do the transfer. In this case, start in the middle of the image and work outwards, being careful not to let the transparency or the fabric move about and smudge the image.

➤ Remove the transparency carefully and hang the fabric up to dry thoroughly - I usually leave on one of the strips of masking tape used to hold the fabric down and use that to hang the fabric from the edge of a shelf. Don't leave the fabric on the Perspex to dry or it will stick and be difficult to remove.

➤ Once the transferred image is thoroughly dry, iron on the back for a couple of minutes with a hot, dry iron to set it. It's then washable.

Aftercare

Medium transfers wash pretty well - the most robust are the ones with a higher proportion of medium to water but the softest are the ones with a higher proportion of water. Make your choices depending on the end use of the fabric.

Moisten the fabric with medium

Smooth the transparency film down

Burnish the image on to the fabric

Check if the transfer is complete

Wash the Perspex and any brushes straight away or the medium will set hard and 'oops there goes another brush!'.

Don't iron directly on to the image - either iron on the back or iron on the front using a piece of baking parchment.

Notes:

➤ You don't, of course, have to transfer the whole of an image - you could deliberately not burnish all over.

➤ At the other end of the scale, if you want to transfer a big image on to fabric but you don't have a wide carriage printer then you can print your image in tiles and transfer your image a section at a time. See the section on Tiling in the chapter on Direct Printing for information on how to do this. Since each tile is on clear transparency film it is easy to see where you need to line up the segments to make a seamless image.

➤ You can dry brush, sponge or screen print the medium on to the fabric for a fractured image. The image will only transfer where the medium is placed, not in the gaps.

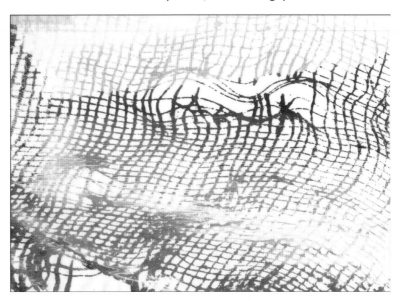

Here I've used a thermofax screen made from a scan of some scrim to print the pattern on to some cotton using textile medium. I then printed the waterscape on to transparency film and transferred it on to the fabric.

As most of the image disappears into the gaps of the pattern, you are left with an impression of the photograph rather than an accurate representation.

Original photograph: Tony Booth

I'm often asked if you can re-use transparency film after a medium transfer. Unfortunately, if you wash inkjet transparency film the coating that gives you the rough surface, that you print on to, comes off. So, you can re-use it for other purposes but not for inkjet printing for medium transfer.

➤ Use opaque screen printing inks instead of colourless medium. I've had some good effects using an opaque white ink which I used on some black linen. I really like the effect of old plaster walls. Of course, you don't have to stick to white ... See an example of this on the next page.

➤ Inkodye extender - I was doing some work on making photographs on fabric using Inkodyes, when I wondered if you could use the clear extender that comes with them to do an inkjet transfer. I tried it with both pigment and dye-based inks. It didn't work with pigment-based inks but did really well with dye-based inks giving a robust transfer. Use it in the same way as a textile medium. Once it's dry it needs to be heated (ironed in a well ventilated area until it stops fuming) or exposed to UV light to make it permanent. I put it under my UV lamp for half an hour and that does the job nicely.

A cornflower transferred on to black linen using opaque screen printing ink.

Original photograph:
Anita Yearsley

This next section is a different way to do a medium transfer and has been around for over 10 years.

The basic process is to:

➤ Print your image on to paper.

➤ Pin or tape your fabric to a firm, flat surface.

➤ Apply an even layer of gel medium to the surface of your print.

➤ Place the print, face down, on to the fabric.

➤ Cover with a paper towel and bray to remove air bubbles and to press the gel into the fabric surface.

➤ Remove the towel and remove any medium left on the paper.

➤ Leave to dry - this is a slow process and can take 24 hours.

➤ Wet the back of the paper, rubbing with a sponge. This will gradually remove the paper, leaving the image on the fabric. After it's dried you may see paper fibres on the surface of the transfer that you missed the first time round - dampen these again and continue rubbing gently to remove them.

I tried this a long time ago and was underwhelmed. I found it time consuming and tedious but I've included it for completeness.

Paper lamination

The last section in this chapter is Paper Lamination. I came across this process on a workshop with Claire Benn and Lesley Morgan at Committed to Cloth. This is really good fun and can produce some beautiful, complex results.

This process can be done using a wide range of imagery from newspaper or magazine images or text (as long as they're not printed on coated papers), to inkjet prints of various sorts, to laser prints. However, since this is a book about digital imagery I'm going to restrict myself to images you can print at home or have printed at a copy shop.

➤ Arrange your printed images, image side up, on to a lightly padded table or bench to form a collage.

➤ Cover your collage with sheer fabric, pinning it tightly to your padded surface so that it doesn't move during the screen printing.

➤ Screen print Liquitex matte medium using your choice of imagery. The design you use on your screen can be pretty much anything. However, if you are using digital printouts then you might like to consider creating a screen or screens from your images by simplifying the image and perhaps changing the scale. The screen then has a visual link to the images you are using for your collage.

➤ Leave the medium to dry thoroughly.

➤ Cover with baking parchment and iron to set the medium. If you forget the baking parchment you'll probably have an iron shaped hole in your work!

➤ Put the whole piece, fabric, paper and all, to soak in a bucket of water for 5 minutes. If you've used dye-based ink don't worry if you get a swoosh of colour in your soaking water. This is just the ink coming off the paper that isn't covered by the medium. Pigment-based ink doesn't do this.

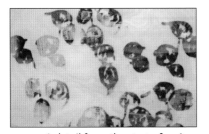

A detail from the start of a piece of lamination created with a thermofax of the 'honesty' plant.

➤ Cover your table with plastic, lay the soaked fabric, paper side up. and rub off the excess paper with either your hands or a pan scrubber - don't put the pulp down the sink! The paper comes away leaving the image on the fabric. Because the fabric is sheer the image can be viewed from either side giving different effects.

➤ Either rinse until the water stays clear or peg the fabric on a washing line and hose it down. I prefer the latter as it's far more fun!

➤ Leave the piece to dry and then review what you want to do next, if anything.

When you are printing your images avoid heavy weight or coated papers - use common or garden 80g cartridge/typing paper. This process will work with laser or inkjet prints but if you are using dye based inks you may find that not all the colour of the print remains after lamination. This is because the inks are laid down in layers. The first colour to be printed attaches itself to the paper most strongly and can come away when the paper is rubbed off

The ink is being laid down in stripes - the cyan is printed first, then the magenta and finally the yellow to complete the image..

The order of colours may be different on different printers.

This is only a taster for this process. I still feel that I am just beginning to appreciate the full potential of this technique for my own work. For a comprehensive guide to lamination, including using metal leaf, as well as a wealth of ideas on how pieces created with lamination can be carried forward, see Committed to Cloth/Art Cloth Studio's book on the subject - details in the Bibliography.

Using Digital Negatives and Positives ...

There are many techniques that I could have included in this section. I decided not to include any technique that required a darkroom as most people reading this book probably don't have one or access to one. If you do then you might like to investigate processes such as Gum Bichromate or Van Dyke prints. Look for books on Alternative Photography and the Alternative Photography web site - www.alternativephotography.com.

Also, I wouldn't personally use some chemicals like silver nitrate in a home environment but would consider using them in my workshop. It is your responsibility to evaluate any chemicals and processes you might want to use and decide if they are suitable for you and your working environment.

DIGITAL POSITIVES AND NEGATIVES

Digital positives are basically ordinary digital images that have been converted to greyscale or black and white and then printed on to transparency film (this used to be called acetate). They are typically used to produce screens for screen printing, such as thermofax screens or photoemulsion screens, or to produce plates for print making, such as solar plates.

A digital negative, on the other hand, like a normal photographic negative, has its tones reversed so black becomes white, white becomes black and so on. It is then printed on to transparency film and is used for contact prints in photographic type methods such as Cyanotyping or Inkodye printing. Some of my favourite Cyanotypes have been made by printing positives rather than negatives - for every rule there's an exception.

Exposure test

All the processes in this section require exposure to a light source of some sort. You may want to do an exposure test to determine how long the exposure needs to be, so I thought I would describe briefly how to do this. The basic procedure is the same whatever your light source.

1. Arrange your light source at right angles to your image. If you are doing an exposure to the sun you may need to prop your board up so it's at the correct angle.

Original photograph

Positive (greyscale) version

Negative version

Photograph by: Robert Hewson

2. Estimate the length of time you think might be suitable for the exposure. The manufacturer of a particular product may give some guidance - Speedball, for instance, give an exposure chart for their photo emulsion using different light sources.
3. Divide this estimate into sections. For instance, using my sunbed to expose cyanotypes I knew that it took something like half an hour. So I divided my test strip into seven strips of five minutes each.
4. I covered the treated fabric and negative except for the first strip, with a piece of card, (anything opaque would do) and swtiched on the sunbed. Every five minutes I moved the card to the next

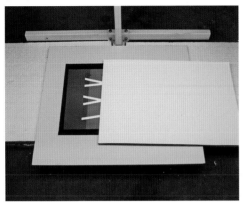 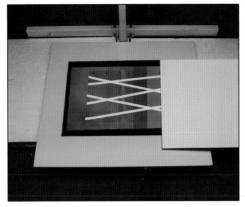

marker. In this way, by the end of the time, the first strip had been exposed for 35 minutes, the next strip had 30, the next 25 and so on. As you can see from the result strip below, the solution on the unexposed strip on the right washed out completely and the fabric returned to white. The strip that was exposed for five minutes gave a pale blue and the colour became progressively darker the longer the exposure went on until it reached 25 minutes. After this there was virtually no colour change, so the exposure time for this light source and this process is 25 minutes.

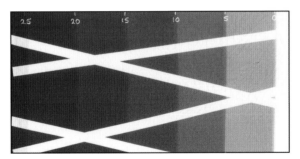

Timings can be affected by several things:

➤ The type of negative you use - I found that negatives printed on tracing paper took approximately 30% longer than ones printed on transparency film and those on oiled paper took around twice the time. These are only rough guidelines as timings will vary depending on the paper and the density of the negative etc.

➤ The distance the light source is from the image - generally the further away the light source, the longer the exposure time that is needed.

➤ Whether you have covered the negative with a sheet of glass or perspex - this may lengthen the exposure needed a little. Be aware that some glass has a built in UV filter and this could lengthen the exposure time a LOT!

You would use a similar method for other processes but how you decide what the right exposure time is will vary. For instance, if you are exposing a photoemulsion screen you are aiming for open areas where your design is, where the ink will go through, and hardened areas elsewhere that will block the ink. So after you have exposed the screen and washed it off, you would look for the best combination of open and closed areas and note the time that was needed to achieve this.

Methods using digital greyscale negatives or positives

The function of a negative or a positive is to act as a sort of resist. Think of sunbathing in a strappy top - your skin changes colour where it is exposed to the sun but the covered areas stay the original colour of your skin. Similarly, light is blocked by dark areas of the negative but light can reach the treated fabric underneath through the clear areas.

The treated areas of the fabric that are exposed to the light react in some way to give you colour or to harden a coating, whereas the treatment on the covered areas usually just washes away.

So, let's start with the greyscale ...

Cyanotypes

I have to admit to a certain fondness for Cyanotyping, sometimes called blueprinting, as I became rather addicted to it and wrote my first book, 'Cyanotypes on Fabric', on the process.

This photographic technique, first developed in the 1840s by the scientist John Herschel, can be used on most natural fibre fabrics (cotton, silk, linen, hemp etc). It is most commonly known as a method for producing photograms. This is where you use small objects, flowers, foliage, lace etc to create the image. Instructions for doing this are in 'Cyanotypes on Fabric', details in the bibliography, which also has instructions for different ways of preparing the fabric for smooth and textured backgrounds, different ways of trapping your design materials, guidance on toning, under and over-dyeing and painting cyanotypes as well as some ideas on combining photograms and photographs.

However, since this is a book on digital imagery, I'm going to concentrate here on cyanotype photographs produced using digital negatives.

So, the first thing is to produce your digital negative. This involves

> converting your image to greyscale

> re-sizing it to fit the transparency film

> increasing the contrast a little and

> inverting the image to give you the negative.

You then print it on to transparency film that is suitable for the type of printer you are using. For detailed instructions on how to do each of these steps, see the chapter on Image Manipulation. You then need to prepare some light-sensitive fabric.

Treat the fabric

First you need to prepare a light sensitive solution. Stir 30g ferric ammonium citrate and 15g potassium ferricyanide in to 250ml of warm water. Both these chemicals are quite safe to use despite their slightly scary names, just take the normal precautions you

There is a process called heliographic or sun printing using fabric paints such as Pebeo transparent/soleil. This is a process using infra red ie heat rather than the ultraviolet light used for cyanotyping.

Although heliographic printing can give some lovely effects, Cyanotyping gives far more detailed, subtle images and can be used with negatives, which is why it's included in this book.

Opposite page:

A combination of two cyanotypes, the top one was produced from a digital negative and the bottom one was produced from a digital positive that had been flipped to mirror the negative.

Original photograph: Lesley Houghton

would use with any powders – don't eat or breathe them in and avoid contact with your skin so that you don't develop a sensitivity to the solution. For further information see the Health and Safety advice in Appendix I, which can also be found on my web site or in my Cyanotype book.

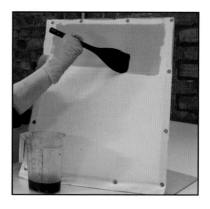

This solution is light sensitive and needs to be stored in a cool, dark place in well-labelled containers. Apply the solution to clean fabric. I think the easiest way to get a smooth, even background is to pin the fabric on a silk painting frame or a picture frame and then paint the solution on to the fabric with even strokes. I use a wide hake brush – these brushes are soft and have no metal parts. You should aim to moisten the fabric with the solution rather than saturate it.

If you don't have a frame you can put the fabric on a sheet of plastic instead. However, if there are any creases in the plastic you will get marks on your fabric as it dries.

The frame is simply there to give you something to hold on to when you move the fabric somewhere dark to dry. A good place to do this is the bottom of an airing cupboard as it's warm and dry. Alternatively you could use a wardrobe or even the shady side of a room. You can speed up the drying process with a hairdryer if you use a low heat and keep it moving but it's quite easy to produce streaks if the heat is concentrated in one place.

When the fabric is dry, you effectively have a photographic plate.

Add the negative or positive
Stage 2 is to lay your digital negative over your dry, treated fabric

Any of you who do rust dyeing need to be aware that the slightest fragment of steel wool etc on your wet cyanotype fabric will make an ugly dark mark which you can't remove.

To get a good image on your fabric you need the negative to be in close contact with the treated fabric. I use two main ways to achieve this depending on the size of print I want to end up with.

➤ If you are using small pieces of fabric then the easiest way I've found is to use a clip frame – this gives you a firm backboard and a piece of glass the right size which already has smooth edges. I put a piece of thin felt or rubber on the backboard, then the treated fabric on top of this. The negative goes on top of the treated fabric, with the right side facing upwards, and the clean glass goes on top of the negative. The clips which come with the clipframe are usually too small when you have several layers to hold together so I use bulldog clips, usually one to each side, which hold the sandwich together in close contact.

➤ The other method I use a lot is to literally stick the negative to the fabric using something like 505 spray or Spraymount. Spray the back of the printed negative rather than the fabric then press firmly on to the fabric.You can buy transparency film for inkjet printers which is already sticky on the back but this is quite expensive and I didn't find it any better than using 505 spray.

505 spray is a temporary adhesive spray designed for use with fabric and is obtainable from most quilt and textile suppliers.

Exposure
Next you need to expose the negative/fabric sandwich to ultra violet (UV) light. To get the sharpest print the light source needs to be perpendicular to the negative/fabric. The most pleasurable way to do this is to use natural sunlight but this can be tricky

Once your fabric is dry, you can keep it out of light by wrapping it up in the light proof blackout fabric used to line blinds and curtains.

Dragonfly shrug

If the piece of fabric you are working on is bigger than your negative then you need to remember that the edges of the digital negatives will usually show on your cyanotype, so you may want to add design elements to disguise the edges or cut your images out of the negative.

For this jacket in silk crepe satin, I printed the negative of the dragonflies on to transparency film in various sizes, cut them out and stuck them to the silk with 505 spray. I then pinned maple leaves round the dragonflies and exposed the whole piece of fabric.

as, if the exposure is lengthy, the sun will have moved. You can also use a sunlamp or sunbed for the exposure which is easier as it is constant in both the amount of UV light it gives off and the direction of the light. So, once you have done a test strip you will know fairly accurately how long you need the exposure to be.

The exposed areas change from the original yellow/green colour through blue to a charcoal grey. So it's fairly easy to tell when an exposure is 'done' just by the colour change.

Just be aware that if you are working on silk you don't always get the grey background, it oftens stays a dark green shade but still changes to Prussian blue when it's rinsed. Also if you are working on viscose the 'white' areas usually stay a creamy colour.

The fully exposed areas of the image are a charcoal grey. As you'll see from the finished version on the next page, these are the areas that become full strength Prussian blue.

The areas here that are dark blue become pale/mid blue.

The yellow/green areas of solution wash away when rinsed and become the original colour of the fabric - in this case white.

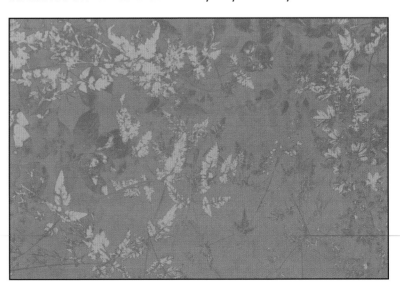

Rinse

Once the exposure is complete, you progress to the final stage, which is to simply keep rinsing the fabric in clean water until the unexposed chemicals wash out and the water remains clear. The exposed areas change from charcoal grey to a vivid Prussian blue and the unexposed areas rinse to white (or whatever the original colour of the fabric was).

The cyanotype will reach its full depth of colour after a few hours but if you want to speed this process up (and I have been known to be slightly impatient at times!) then use a small glug of (3%) hydrogen peroxide to the final rinse water. I suppose this is something like a tablespoon to 5 litres/a gallon of water.

Looking after your cyanotypes

You have to remember that cyanotypes are produced using a photographic process not a dye and that they are susceptible to three things, abrasion, contact with alkalies and sunlight.

Abrasion - cyanotypes probably aren't suitable for something which is going to receive a lot of rubbing. The colour sits on the surface of the fabric so, in the same way that indigo is rubbed off the seams of jeans, the colour of a cyanotype can be abraded over time.

Alkalies - cyanotypes can be washed but you need to be very careful what you wash them with. Avoid soap and normal detergents; instead look for something designed to wash silk or wool. Other things you could try are baby shampoo or some washing up liquids. The main things are to use the minimum quantity possible and to test your liquid BEFORE you try it on your art work. Once you've lost the colour through contact with alkali you cannot get it back. Also remember the above comments about abrasion so use a gentle swishing movement rather than a rubbing action when you are washing them.

If you live in a hard water area, so the water itself is alkaline, then you might like to add a splash of vinegar to your final rinse. Where

> Do make sure that you rinse until the water runs clear and then give it one more rinse. If any of the solution is left in the fabric then, over time, the white areas of your image may develop a pale blue colour as the residual solution reacts with any available UV light.

I live, it is enough to leave a cyanotype in plain tap water over night for the colour to be bleached out!

Sunlight - the third thing to be aware of is that If you leave a cyanotype in the sun then the print will fade over time but cyanotypes have a fascinating property – if you put them somewhere dark most of the colour will return. What happens is that the Prussian blue is converted by the UV light to Prussian white which makes the image look faded. Over time the Prussian white will re-oxidise back to Prussian blue and the image is restored. Don't you wish you could do that with your hand-dyed fabrics!

You may like to spray your finished work with something like Scotchguard or another UV protective spray. Just make sure you test anything new on a scrap piece of cyanotyped fabric just to make sure it isn't going to damage your work. Also bear in mind that anything you put in contact with your cyanotype may damage it in the long term. Mike Ware's book (see Bibliography) has a very comprehensive and technical explanation of the chemistry and preservation issues for cyanotypes.

* * * * *

On the next two pages are a unique pair of quilts made using the cyanotype process with digital negatives

by Cathy Corbishley Michel.

There is a lovely description of using Inkodyes to produce photograms in Carolyn A Dahl's book 'Transforming Fabric' – she has such joy in her work and it comes through in her writing. In fact, it was Carolyn's book that introduced me to Inkodyes in the first place.

Inkodye Prints

Inkodyes are little known in the UK – they are very concentrated vat dyes and the end result is probably as stable as anything that can be achieved at home, being able to withstand hot washing, bleach and abrasion. They are translucent, so the underlying colour/pattern will show through, and they don't stiffen the fabric.

The manufacturers only specify that they can be used with cellulose based fabrics such as cotton and linen; I've successfully used them on silk and other fibres but I don't know what the long term stability will be.

Inkodyes can be used for a wide range of methods from direct painting, screen printing and stamping to tie-dye and batik. They can also be used to produce a light sensitive fabric, in a similar way to cyanotype solution, which can then be exposed with a digital negative to produce an image.

If you've ever produced cyanotypes then you'll find this process very familiar as it follows the same sequence – prepare the fabric with a light sensitive liquid, add a negative, expose to UV light and wash.

This evocative pair of quilts were designed and created by Cathy Corbishley Michel based on original photographs taken on the ill-fated Ernest Shackleton Expedition to the Antarctic.

I asked Cathy to tell the story of how the quilt came to be made in her own words.

Endurance 1, The Endurance and the James Caird - 64" x 44"

I became interested in the Ernest Shackleton's Endurance Expedition to Antarctica (1914-16) after seeing the famous picture of the ship stuck in the ice taken by Frank Hurley in Midwinter 1915. The ship subsequently sank and Shackleton and his crew had a remarkable escape after drifting on the icepack and then taking to the sea in open boats. The quality of the black and white pictures and the character of the ship and crew in the icy landscape lent themselves to Cyanotype printing. I obtained permission to use the images in my work from the Royal Geographical Society (who hold the glass plate negatives) and the Scott Polar Research Institute (who have an album of photographs).

The images were scanned from purchased photographic prints and publications and converted in Photoshop to high contrast negatives before printing onto either A3 or A4 acetates using either a laser or inkjet printer, or in the case of the larger negatives, an A3 photocopier. The negatives had occasional scratches or errors on them from the printing jets or rollers of the photocopier which I carefully edited with a fine pointed black permanent felt pen. I initially wanted to print the images on fine linen, but eventually settled for good quality recycled cotton sheets which I cut into pieces of at least A3 size, impregnated with Cyanotype chemicals and hung to dry in a darkroom.

When dry, the fabric was carefully ironed, laid onto a flat surface with the negatives on top and weighted down by sheets of glass to ensure good contact. It was then exposed to UV light for 25-30 minutes using an old sunbed canopy purchased second-hand for £25. The finished prints were rinsed thoroughly in tap

Endurance 2, *Shackleton and his Men - 64" x 44*

water but given a final wash in the washing machine (after cleaning out all traces of alkaline detergents) using a very small amount of white vinegar in the final rinse to ensure an acid environment to preserve the colour. The same method was used to wash the final quilts. Any small marks or errors in the prints were carefully touched up using a combination of fine blue permanent marker or pencil with white chinagraph pencil on the dry completed quilt.

Initially I was intending only to print pictures of the ship and the small boats and icy landscapes but as I read about the extraordinary survival story of the 28 men over their 2 year ordeal I began to appreciate their skills and characters so I also printed a number of the Hurley crew portraits, including a 19 year old stowaway and the Ship's cat (the latter did not survive) and the autographed banjo now in the National Maritime museum in Greenwich. The process of watching the pictures of the ship and the ice and the life-size faces of the men emerging from the rinse process was highly evocative.

The pictures were trimmed and assembled into two large quilts with a positive and negative print of the Ship in the Ice as centrepieces. They were sandwiched with Warm and Natural white 2oz cotton wadding and then backed with cotton sheeting before quilting on a domestic Bernina 630 sewing machine using hand guided free machine quilting with Rayon 40wt Madeira threads in blue and pale grey. I used an over large vermicelli type pattern changing thread colour to tone in with the background of the pictures. The quilt was bound with surplus reject prints on cotton cut into 2 and a half inch widths and sewn together to make double fold binding. The final washing process caused the wadding to shrink slightly and gave additional surface texture. After drying the surface of the quilts was coated with fabric protector to prevent damage during exhibition and transit. The pair of quilts was hung as part of an exhibition at the Royal College of Pathologists in central London over the summer of 2010 - Cathy Corbishley Michel

Prepare the fabric

The dye as it comes out of the bottle is, surprisingly, a pale, creamy slightly greyish liquid irrespective of the colour it will develop into, except the yellow, which is pale yellow in the bottle. This makes judging the strength of colour a bit tricky. If you want to dilute the colour you achieve, you can either dilute the dye with water or with the extender sold with the dye but since we are not worried here about maintaining the thickness of the dye, water is cheaper.

This is one time I would definitely recommend that you make notes as you go along and keep records of the dilution and the fabric used as well as the exposure time and development method.

I think the easiest way to apply the dye, if you want a smooth background, is to pin your fabric on to something like a silk painting frame and paint the dye on with a large soft brush, using even strokes. You can also apply the dye in various ways to give a textured background in the same way that you can with cyanotype solution. Try sponging it on or dry brushing it. You can also try applying the dye and then scrunching it and leaving it to dry. The creases in the fabric give a faint crystalline effect to the background.

The fabric now needs to be left to dry somewhere dark or in subdued light. A good place to do this is the bottom of an airing cupboard as it's warm, dry and dark. Alternatively you could use a wardrobe or even the shady side of a room.

When you are using Inkodyes with a negative you develop the colour using UV light but when you are using other processes the colour can be developed by using heat, usually using an iron or by baking, so I assumed that I couldn't speed up the process by drying the fabric with a hairdryer. I found that I could if I used a low heat and kept it moving– I assume that the hairdryer doesn't get hot enough to start the colour change but do test your own dryer before you try it with a large piece.

Add the negative or positive

Place your digital negative or positive, right side up, over your dry, treated fabric.

To get a good image on your fabric you need the negative to be in close contact with the treated fabric. I use two main ways to achieve this depending on the size of print I want to end up with.

➤ If you are using small pieces of fabric then the easiest way I've found is to use a clip frame – this gives you a firm backboard and a piece of glass the right size which already has smooth edges. I put a piece of thin felt or rubber on the backboard, then the treated fabric on top of this. The negative goes on top of the treated fabric and the clean glass goes on top of the negative. The clips which come with the clipframe are usually too small when you have several

If you are planning to screen print or stamp with Inkodyes then it would be better to use the extender to make the dyes paler as it maintains a good consistency for these processes.

There is some very useful information on Inkodyes, and their varied uses and methods on the Dharma Trading Company web site - www.dharmatrading. com

As the dye is pale it is very easy to miss splashes of it when you are cleaning up. You will certainly notice them when they have developed! So, either work in an area that will be improved by some odd splashes of vivid colour or put down newspapers or plastic sheeting before you start.

layers to hold together so I use bulldog clips, usually one to each side, which hold the sandwich together in close contact.

➤ The other method I use a lot is to literally stick the negative to the fabric using something like 505 spray or Spraymount. Spray the back of the printed negative rather than the fabric then press firmly on to the fabric. You can buy transparency film for inkjet printers which is already sticky on the back but this is quite expensive and I didn't find it any better than using 505 spray.

Exposure

Next you need to expose the negative/fabric sandwich to ultra violet (UV) light. To get the sharpest print the light source needs to be perpendicular to the negative/fabric. The most pleasurable way to do this is to use natural sunlight but this can be tricky as, if the exposure is lengthy, the sun will have moved. You can also use a sunlamp or sunbed for the exposure which is easier as it is constant in both the amount of UV light it gives off and the direction of the light. So, once you have done a test strip you will know fairly accurately how long you need the exposure to be.

You judge the exposure by the change of colour – when it's the colour you want, take it out of the UV light and wash immediately.

After treatment

Wash thoroughly after exposure to remove unexposed dye. Some pale coloration may remain in the unexposed areas ie it may not revert completely to the original colour of the fabric, but I think that's part of its charm.

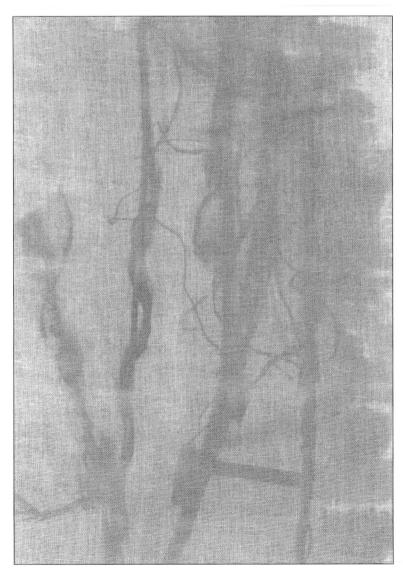

This image shows an Inkodye print where the dye has been applied with a dry brush. The negative was made by scanning some hairy string and then converting it using the instructions in the chapter on Image Manipulation.

METHODS USING BLACK AND WHITE DIGITAL NEGATIVES OR POSITIVES

Screen printing basics

Most people are familiar, to some extent, with screen printing where you have mesh stretched over a frame of some sort, often made of wood. A design is applied to the mesh so that some of it is covered and some is left open. Ink or another medium is pushed through the open holes in the mesh with a squeegee to create a design on the fabric, paper or other substrate.

Traditionally printers have used silk screens to produce wonderfully detailed fine art prints by preparing an image in a series of layers, each layer being achieved by a separate layer of ink or other media The screen had to be lined up accurately, known as registration, for each layer of the print.

In modern textile work a simpler, more spontaneous way of working has been promoted by Jane Dunnewold in the USA and Committed to Cloth in the UK where a screen is used as a means of repeating an image multiple times on a piece of cloth. Different coloured inks/paints can be used to vary the image and the screen can be used in different orientations for further variety but the method primarily involves a single print of the screen for each image so no registration is needed.

All sorts of media can be used with these screens – try dye paints, textile paints, screenprinting inks, discharge paste, devore paste, glue (for foiling), gutta and so on

The surface you print on affects the quality of the print you can achieve on fabric. Aim for a lightly padded surface. To get started you can use an old blanket or towel with a sheet over the top but if you get into this, and it can be thoroughly addictive, you will probably want to make a larger surface. I use a piece of mdf a bit bigger than my table, covered with two layers of felt and a piece of cotton loomstate. These are each stapled tightly over the mdf. When I print I then cover the surface with a drop cloth (usually another piece of cotton loomstate). The drop cloth absorbs any excess media that goes through the fabric you are printing and helps prevent smearing. When I'm not printing the board can stand up against the wall.

The fabric you are printing on is pinned through the drop cloth into the padded surface so that it doesn't lift up when you raise the screen after you've made a print.

To get started put a fat bead of media along one edge of the inside of the screen. Pull the media towards you over the surface of the mesh,, with a squeegee, keeping the squeegee more or less upright. and maintaining even pressure. The media is then squeezed through the open parts of the mesh to form the design on the fabric.

I'm going to describe fairly briefly three ways to produce printing screens based on digital imagery - photoemulsion, thermofax and

Since this book is about digital images on fabric I've restricted this section to screens made from digital negatives and photoemulsion but there are many other ways to make screens. I can thoroughly recommend Jane Dunnewold's book 'Improvisional Screen Printing' and 'Screen Printing - Layering textiles with colour, texture and imagery' by Clare Benn and Leslie Morgan.

A number of these improvisational techniques use a temporary design on the screen. They can result in gorgeous, spontaneous images which break down as the prints are made. However, if you get one that you want to make a lot of prints from or which you want to keep for future use, you can scan one of your prints and make it into a permanent screen using the photoemulsion technique, a Thermofax screen or a PhotoEZ screen.

Don't worry if you aren't printing in black as the colour can be changed once it's been scanned or photographed - see the chapter on Image Manipulation. I find this a lovely way to work as you can use the spontaneity and serendipity of a fleeting technique but can then capture the result for future use.

For speed I'm going to refer to digital positives in the next few sections - just remember that you could also use a black and white negative, in which case you would print the background around the image rather than the image itself.

photoEze screens. All of these basically require a black and white image - after all mesh is either open or closed - ink can either go through or it can't. The mesh is very fine so to some extent screens can simulate tonal images but I've been most pleased by screens that have been converted from greyscale to a black and white image befoe I've made the screens. There are various methods of doing this in the chapter on Image Manipulation. Not all work well with all images - you may need to experiment a little.

Photoemulsion Screens

Photoemulsion screens can produce very finely detailed imagery so work particularly well with digital positives. They require little equipment but do need a dark area for drying the light sensitive coating.

Preparing a photoemulsion screen involves five steps;

➤ Produce your digital positive and print it on to transparency film.

➤ Coat your screen with the prepared emulsion and dry it in the dark.

➤ Place the positive over the dried surface.

➤ Expose the screen to light.

➤ Finally, wash the screen with a jet of water. Where the screen has been exposed to the light the emulsion will have hardened but where it has been covered up it remains soft and washes away, revealing the screen mesh.

Prepare your digital positive
If you haven't done this before, just follow the instructions in the chapter on Image Manipulation.

Prepare the screen
➤ Make sure the screen is clean and free of oil/grease – if necessary clean with household cleaner and a brush. This is especially important with new screens. Dry the screen thoroughly.

Note that the bottle of sensitiser has a little pad inside the lid. When you remove the lid to add the water make sure this pad doesn't fall out or you might get solution leaking down the bottle when you shake it.

➤ Prepare the photoemulsion following the manufacturer's instructions. The Speedball diazo system, which is the one I use, comes in two bottles. There is a small one that appears virtually empty and a bigger one that contains a thick blue fluid. You ¾ fill the little bottle with water and shake it with enthusiasm until the contents are dissolved. You then tip this solution into the contents of the bigger bottle and stir it until thoroughly mixed, at which point it has turned green. It's then ready to use. The sensitised emulsion has quite a good shelf life - Speedball say 4 weeks at 70°F, 8 weeks at 70°F and 4 months in a fridge.

➤ The emulsion is now heat/light sensitive but, like cyanotype solution, you don't need to work in a darkroom or use a safety light, just work in subdued normal light.

➤ Squeegee an even layer over the back of the screen, the flat side. This does require a little practice as, if the layer is too thick the light can't penetrate all the way through and doesn't harden properly when you expose it. If the emulsion is too thin you may get bits of mesh that aren't covered when it has dried. Turn the screen over and squeegee off any surplus emulsion that has come through.

➤ Dry the coated screen horizontally in a dark place with the back of the screen towards the floor, propped up on little blocks or jars so that air can flow round the screen and aid the drying process. This is the bit that seems to put people off. There are several options. I often put screens underneath a table and drape the sides with blackout fabric, often sold for lining household blinds/curtains. I've also used the bottom of the airing cupboard as it is warm and dark.

➤ The screen is now ready to use.

> *My airing cupboard rarely has clothes in it - it's too full of other stuff drying!*

3. Add your digital positive.

The traditional way seems to be to place your digital positive, image side up, on the inside of the screen, over the treated surface and to then place a piece of glass over the negative inside the screen to hold it in close contact. However, if you do it this way you need a piece of glass for pretty much each size of screen. So, I turn my screen upside down ie the flat side uppermost, I place my negative on top, right side down, and put a piece of glass over the top to hold the negative in place. One biggish piece of glass then pretty much 'does all'.

I put this upside down sandwich on a piece of black felt to stop light sneaking up round the edges and do the exposure.

3. Expose the screen

You can use various light sources to expose a photoemulsion screen ranging from Photoflood bulbs to a sunbed. Received wisdom is that you use a 250w BBA photoflood bulb suspended above the surface on which you will have your screen. The guideline is that the distance from the light source should be something like the diagonal of the screen, if you want somewhere to start. If you are preparing a big screen and you have the light source too close the edges may not get enough light and won't expose correctly.

Speedball give a chart of suggested timings for two different bulbs:

150 Watt Bulb, Clear Incandescent

Screen Size . 150W Bulb Height . . Exposure Time

8"x10" . . . .12 inches . . . .45 minutes

10"x14" . . . .12 inches . . . .45 minutes

12"x18" . . . .15 inches . . . . 1 hr. 14 minutes

16"x20 . . . .17 inches . . . . 1 hr. 32 minutes

18"x20" . . . .17 inches . . . . 1 hr. 32 minutes

BBA No. 1 Photoflood (250 Watt)

Screen Size . . Lamp Height . . Exposure Time

8" x 10". . . . . . 12 inches . . . . . 10 minutes

10"x14". . . . . . 12 inches . . . . . 10 minutes

12 "x 18" . . . . .15 inches . . . . . 16 minutes

16"x20" . . . . . 17 inches . . . . 20 minutes

18"x20" . . . . . 17 inches . . . . . 20 minutes

Note:

➤ These timings assume you are using a foil pie plate above your bulb to act as a reflector.

➤ The photoflood bulb can get pretty hot - you probably won't be able to use it in a normal lamp fitting. Ask where you bought the photoflood bulb from what they would recommend.

I didn't have a photoflood bulb when I started to do these screens so I used my trusty sunbed. It worked fine and all I had to do was an exposure test to see how long I needed to leave the screens under for.

4. Wash the screen

Using a fairly strong water spray, wash the exposed screen. Unexposed emulsion should be washed away, opening the screen.

Allow the screen to dry thoroughly and it is then ready to print with.

Notes:

➤ Wash the screen out as soon as you've finished printing so that the ink or other media doesn't dry in the screen and block the mesh. Dry the screen and store upright.

➤ If the emulsion washes away after washing then there could be a number of reasons.

　　》 The exposure was too short – try a longer exposure or alter the distance between the light source and the emulsion

　　》 The screen was greasy before the emulsion was applied

　　》 The emulsion wasn't properly dried before the exposure

　　》 The emulsion may have been too old.

　　》 Your negative may not have been dark enough to block the light out. The emulsion will start to harden underneath and it won't wash out properly. Ways round this are to darken your negative or print two negatives and use them together.

To re-use the screen simply soak it in bleach and the emulsion will come off. Do make sure you do this in a sensible place, ie it is well ventilated and away from pets and children. Don't stand and watch it ...!

PhotoEZ

PhotoEZ is a sort of ready-made equivalent of a photoemulsion screen but without some of the fuss. I haven't used these for very long, but I think they are rather intriguing.

There is no coating to apply, the sheets come ready to use with a protective plastic covering sheet. You simply lay down a sheet of black plastic or fabric, remove the protective film from the photoEZ and place it, shiny side up, on top. Then you add your digital positive, image side up, and finish by adding a sheet of glass or perspex (plexiglass) to finish the sandwich.

The film is then exposed to light. The timing depends on the type of light source and how far it is away from the film. EZScreenprint suggests 1 min in bright sun and I needed about 10 minutes on my elderly sunbed. The time will need to be extended if you are using anything other than transparency flm for your positive, such as thin paper. There really is no substitute for doing an exposure test, described at the beginning of this chapter.

Soak the exposed film in water for 10-15 minutes. Lay it on a piece of plastic canvas or similar and rinse with a spray. The area that has been covered up stays soft and rinses away so the mesh is exposed, whereas the areas that were exposed to the light have hardened and remain. You can help things along by brushing gently with a soft brush.

Once you've patted your film dry, expose it to your light source again to finish drying and harden. Then go and print.

This is a very brief introduction to this process - if you are interested, go and have a look at the EZScreenPrint web site, www.ezscreenprint.com, or Ginny Eckley's site, www.photoezsilkscreen.com. There is a wealth of information and instruction on both sites.

> *You may find it easier to print if you fix your film to a frame of some sort, like the thin plastic ones sold for use with thermofax screens. I think you get crisper images if the film is supported when you are printing.*

Thermofax

I first came across thermofax screens at a workshop at Committed to Cloth in the UK. We used them to repeat images on a large piece of fabric as one stage of producing art cloth. For me this was 'the missing link', something that would let me combine easily digital images with screen printing.

Thermal imagers, or thermofax machines, used to be used for making office stencils before photocopiers became more common. They have now been adopted by textile artists (and tattoo artists, but that's another story!) as a method of creating very detailed printing screens. Basically, art work is printed on to paper, this is sandwiched with the special mesh and is passed through the machine. The coating on the mesh is burnt

An A4 Panenka thermal imager

A wall hanging created from a series of thermofax screens. Each element was made from either a simplified digital photograph such as the dandelion heads and the ivy down the sides or from a scanned item like the torn hessian at the bottom, the grasses and the feather.. Each screen was used multiple times, varying the colours to give variety and depth to the hanging.

away in the areas where there is artwork, leaving the mesh open.

Mesh and frame types
The mesh used to create the thermofax stencils is made up of a polyester mesh with a plastic coating on one side. It comes in two main mesh sizes 70 and 100 (a finer mesh). For printing on fabric I use the 70.

Preparing images and printer/photocopier considerations
It is usually said that you need a laser printer/photocopier to produce the artwork for a thermofax screen. I am lucky enough to have access to quite a range of printers and this certainly isn't the case now – inkjet printers using pigment based inks often work well but dye based inks usually don't.

The image you want to use is printed on to paper.

There are a few things that are specific to preparing the images for thermofax screens. If you are printing with a laser printer the important thing is that you only want the minimum of toner on your paper ie your image should look pale. There are several methods you can use; firstly, if your printer has an economy mode then try that - consult your printer's manual for information on how to do this. If this doesn't give you a pale enough image then look and see if there is a draft mode - this may roughen the image but it's worth trying.

My favourite method is to reduce the opacity of your image in Elements. I found that 40% worked on my colour laser printer but I needed to reduce it to 30% for my mono printer. The amount you need to reduce the opacity will vary depending on the image and your printer. Very fine lines can be darker than bigger areas of black. If there is too much toner/ink, too much heat will be generated in the machine and the mesh may warp.

Adding the positive
The mesh is placed on top of the positive with the shiny side facing the image. The sandwich is then fed through the machine.The image is burnt through the plastic coating leaving the mesh open.

If you are making a small screen (A5 or less) then you might want to use a carrier. This is made up of two pieces of laser transparency film taped together at the short end to make a hinge. The image and film go inside the carrier which helps it feed smoothly through the thermofax machine. NB DO NOT use inkjet transparency film in a thermofax machine as it is not designed to withstand the heat produced and will probably melt inside. NOT a good idea.

When the sandwich has cooled pull the mesh away from the artwork a little way and hold it up to the light. You should be able to see through the image. As Guenther Panenka described it, when you pull the mesh away from the artwork it should sound right – it shouldn't stick but should sound 'crisp'.

> *If you manage to buy your own machine then I suggest you consult the Committed to Cloth book, 'Thermofax Printing, Bringing personal imagery alive', for guidance on all things thermofax*

> *When I started to write this book I was going to give a list of printers that did and didn't work but ink formulations and printer models are changing so quickly the list would have been out of date before the book was printed.*

Thermofax mesh mounted in a plastic frame and duct taped.

A selection of thermofax designs

Mounting mesh in frame

It's possible to print with a thermofax taped round the edges with duct tape but it's easier to handle if it's taped to a plastic frame which can be bought specifically for this purpose. You could also tape the mesh to a set of canvas stretchers.

Thermofax screens can be used either side up but the shiny side isn't as tough as the matte side so you'll need to be more careful you don't damage it. You can reverse the image on your computer very easily to produce a mirror image and then burn another screen.

Follow the general instructions earlier in this chapter for how to use and care for your printing screens. You will need to use a lighter squeegee than usual for your thermofaxes. I use a grout spreader from my local hardware store - it has a thin, flexible rubber blade that i find just right.

How to care for screens

The usual precautions apply, so wash your thermofax, before the media dries, with a soft brush or sponge. Don't use anything abrasive as it may damage the surface.

I'd like to finish this chapter by mentioning one more technique. I've been experimenting with something called solar plate. This is made up of a thin sheet of photopolymer film bonded to a metal sheet. The method is very similar to using photoemulsion or photoEZ. You place a positive over the film and expose it to UV light. You then wash it. The film that has been exposed to UV light has hardened and where it's been covered up it remains soft and can be washed away.

I don't know enough about this technique yet to write about it in any depth but you may like to experiment with this process to produce either printing or rubbing plates from your digital images.

There is a book by Welden & Muir on this subject in the Bibliography or you could try one of the excellent courses run by the Sidney Nolan Trust,

http://www.sidneynolantrust.org

Image Manipulation ...

GETTING YOUR IMAGES IN

The whole process starts with getting a digital image into your computer and there are several methods for capturing digital images ready for your imagination to work on. Scanning is a very easy, surprisingly versatile method but the first one most people would think of is using a digital camera.

For those of us old enough to have used film cameras for many years the first time using a digital camera is quite a culture shock. Instead of waiting to finish a film off, take it somewhere to be developed and printed and then see what you've got, you can take a picture with a digital camera and view it straight away on the camera's screen to get a rough idea of how good it is. Then, all you need to do to see it in all its glory is to plug the camera into your computer and there it is on the screen ready for you to change the size, cut out areas you don't like, change the contrast and so on (once you've learned how, of course). As I'd worked in IT for 20 years or so, I fell instantly in love with digital photography and have had great fun learning and working out how to incorporate digital imagery into my textile work.

The specifications of digital cameras are changing so rapidly at the moment that anything I write here will be out of date before it's printed! So, all I really want to say is use what you have and take lots of pictures. We're going to be using our images on fabric and none of the techniques require a very high resolution image to look good. If you really get into all this and you are dissatisfied with the quality of your images then you can research and buy something better later on. The only thing that is rarely mentioned in the 'What to buy' guides is the physical size of the camera - does the camera feel comfortable in your hands? Can you reach the button, especially the shutter button, without changing your grip on the camera. If possible, go into a good camera shop and try holding various cameras as you would when taking a picture and see what feels good to you. I have small hands and some cameras felt clumsy to me.

I think here is the place to point out that I'm NOT a trained photographer. I am an enthusiastic amateur and have taught myself from books and experience what will work for me.

I've included books in the Bibliography on the technicalities of digital photography but also some of my favourites on the creative side of digital photography.

As a non-professional photographer I have learned how F-stops and shutter speed work together to give a particular exposure or depth of field but it takes me a while to work things out sometimes – I don't do enough for it to be instinctive - so I went for a camera that would work pretty much on its own, using the fully automatic setting, when I'm in a rush but would also give me fine control when I need it using the various semi-automatic or manual settings.

Tips on taking photographs

When I was working out what to include in this book I decided the main focus would be on how to use digital imagery with textiles plus some guidance and ideas on how you can prepare and manipulate those images, but that the technicalities of how to take photographs would be best left in more capable hands. So, I've just given a few suggestions here ...

➤ Watch what is in the background – a lot can be done at the editing stage but starting with a decent photograph in the first place is easier. One very simple tip is if you are taking a picture of, say, a specimen flower then slip a piece of contrasting card behind the flower so if you want to remove the background in the photograph later it will be much easier.

➤ Don't miss a picture through dithering – one of the joys of digital photography is that you can take lots of pictures and simply discard anything you don't like. However, don't discard an image simply because it isn't technically a 'good' photograph. There is a section in Charlotte Ziebarth's book (see Bibliography) which is a masterclass on taking simple images, in this case birds, from very mediocre pictures and manipulating them in a variety of ways to make stunning quilts.

➤ Try taking pictures from a variety of angles. Getting down to ground level and looking up or getting a high viewpoint and looking down on your subject can often give you gorgeous patterns and textures you might otherwise miss.

➤ If you are not sure which part of a scene to take, take it all – you can always crop it later. Then zoom in and take some detail shots.

➤ Generally speaking take your pictures at the highest resolution your camera will allow. This gives you the most options should you wish to print the image at a large size. Higher resolution images take up more hard disk than low resolution ones so, the downside is that you will be able to store fewer pictures in your camera's memory. Memory cards are now pretty cheap so you may want to buy a spare.

Tips for holding your camera steady and avoiding blurry images:

➤ Keep elbows in to your sides

➤ Hold your breath while pressing the shutter

➤ Lean against something

➤ Support your camera on a bean bag to keep it steady or use a tripod with a cable or electronic shutter release..

Of course, you don't always want a sharp image. Try deliberately moving the camera while you are taking a picture or use a very slow exposure with a moving subject and see if you like the blurred effects.

Downloading your images

Once the images are on your camera's memory card they need to be transferred (downloaded) to your computer so you can have fun with them.

The most common way to do this is to attach the camera to your computer via the cable that came with your it, most commonly a USB cable although some high-end cameras use a faster firewire connection. Look at the documentation that came with your camera to see what procedure you need to follow to download your pictures.

Alternatively, you can buy a card reader that connects directly to your computer. You simply take the memory card out of your camera and put it in the card reader. Some printers have a card reader built into them so you can print directly from the memory card, but then you lose the creative part of using a computer.

If you already use a memory stick (pen drive) you will be familiar with how they appear on your computer when you insert one into a USB port. You normally see your regular drives with their associated letter. So, for instance, your main hard disk is your C: drive, your CD or DVD drive is often D: and so on. Removable drives, like a memory stick, usually take temporary letters from the end of the alphabet so your camera or card reader may well appear as Z: drive. The photos on the memory card will then appear as files which you can copy across in the usual way to a folder on your computer.

Alternatively you may have software on your computer, like Photoshop Elements downloader, which detects when you connect your camera and will download all or selected pictures to your computer, often creating folders for you at the same time.

USING A SCANNER

Why would you use a scanner instead of a digital camera? Well, I see them as a pair of allies who complement rather than replace each other. If you want to capture something flat, like a map, then the easiest way is to scan it as the scanner provides even lighting for your image so that's something you don't have to worry about.

I'm not going to cover drum or slide scanners, just flat bed scanners which are the ones normally used at home and in small businesses.

Scanning involves putting an image or object on the clear, flat surface of the scanner, called the 'bed'. An arm with a row of sensors, called a linear array, and a light source passes over the bed in small steps capturing rows of images that are then put together to make a digital image that can be displayed on and manipulated by your computer.

If you are reading the specification of a scanner the resolution is usually given by two numbers, eg 1200 x 2400. The first of these numbers is the number of sensors on the arm and the second is the number of steps the arm takes over the bed. Think of it as a grid of sensors and steps with each sensor/step becoming a pixel of your image. This is the true or optical resolution of your scanner.

Each sensor is called an SPD (silicon photo diode) and together they make up a linear CCD (charged couple device) – I think I've glazed over at this point. I don't understand exactly how these work but it hasn't held me back yet .....

See Michael Freeman's book for more technical information – he gives very clear explanations of terms like dynamic range, noise and bit depth. See the bibliography for details.

Before you start a scan make sure the bed of the scanner is clean – look at the documentation that came with your scanner and see what they recommend as a cleaner. If you've lost the documentation, you could try looking on the manufacturer's web site to see if you can find out. I find the wipes sold for cleaning your monitor are good for this purpose but they may not be suitable for your scanner.

Manufacturers often give another set of figures for the digital resolution of the scanner, sometimes ambiguously referred to as the 'maximum' resolution. In order to give the illusion of higher resolution, the scanner software takes the optical resolution and tries to guess or interpolate what the necessary additional pixels would be in terms of colour and brightness. This is called interpolation and can be done in your image editing software just as well if not better, so ignore that bit of the specification.

Most of the digital photography books I've read talk about scanners in terms of scanning small negatives or slides with a view to printing them as photographs later. This process usually requires scanning at a very high resolution in order to be able to expand the image at a high printing resolution. For textile work, we are more likely to be interested in the effect of the image rather than whether it is pin sharp or not, so we therefore have much more modest requirements in terms of hardware. Virtually any home scanner will give you many, many options. So, before you are tempted to upgrade your equipment, play around with what you have and see if you like the results.

If you are going to be scanning anything other than paper documents I would recommend you put a piece of transparency film over the bed of your scanner to protect it. I have been known to get carried away and start scanning something like a juicy slice of lemon and then think …

Scanners usually have a menu of options you can choose from. This may be in the form of a window on the machine itself with buttons to allow you to move between the options and to select, or it may be in the software on your computer. It looks a bit like the printer options dialogue box which lets you select the type of paper you are going to print on etc. The scanner dialogue will offer you options like the resolution you are going to scan at. I would suggest that for general use you scan at 300dpi. However, if you are scanning something very small, eg a 2" x 2.5" print, that you know you are going to print at a much larger size, eg A4 then scan at, say, 600 dpi.

Depending on the make and the model you may also have options to invert the image (to produce a negative) , to change the size of the image etc.

So, what can you scan? The obvious things are flat documents like photographic prints, text, maps, drawings, fabric, etc, but you can also scan 3D objects like flowers, or grasses. If you leave the lid of the scanner up then you can experiment with anything that will fit on the scanner and not damage it – try pieces of wood or stone or perhaps some hairy string. Try scanning translucent items like bubble wrap or a cut glass bowl, or how about cutting thin slices of fruit such as lemons or vegetables such as courgettes or tomatoes…. What about scanning rice grains at a high resolution and then blowing the image up. Try placing objects between layers of transparent fabrics.

You can use a piece of fabric, crumpled tissue or cling film, or hand-made paper over the objects you are scanning to give a background.

If you really get into the creative use of a scanner you may want to construct a shallow box that you can use to give yourself an even background that you can change without putting any pressure on the items you are trying to capture. You may also want to construct some mechanism so that you can support items such as delicate flowers, on the surface of the scanner without them being flattened.

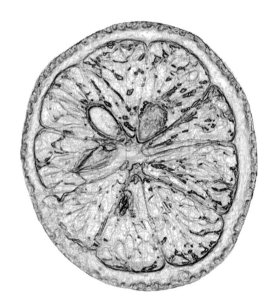

A slice of lemon, scanned and then converted to a black and white image ready to make a thermofax screen.

Storing and Organising Your Images

If you end up with a lot of images you can use something like the Organiser in Elements to categorise them. This sort of software allows you to assign keywords to an image such as, perhaps, a date, the location where it was taken or a subject. At a later date you can search for images based on the keywords.

If you don't want to spent time just now learning how to use the Organiser then I would suggest you make folders for your original images and give them logical names. When you want to work on an image, make a working copy and put it in a project folder. That way, if you make a real, um, mess of things you can go back to the original and make a fresh working copy, although the Undo History will get you out of most things - see later in the chapter. It's amazing how liberating this little procedure can be, especially if you are new to this way of working or new to a particular piece of software. It doesn't matter if you get things wrong – just start again with a new copy.

MANIPULATING YOUR IMAGES

What I'm trying to do in this section is to give you some ideas on how you can use software to manipulate your images into a form that works well in textile work and to give you some pointers on how this might be done.

I'm assuming you know how to use the basic facilities on your computer as it's outside the scope of this book to teach basic computer skills. However, I can give you a few pointers that may help you make the best use of your equipment and software and also, hopefully, clarify some confusing terminology.

What I can't do is give you a detailed sequence of steps for your particular software, unless you are using Photoshop Elements v8. You will need to do some investigating with either a good manual and/or the help system on your software. I wll try and tell you where you are likely to find particular functions or tools.

SOFTWARE

In order to manipulate digital images you will need some image editing software. There are many different varieties of this ranging from the all-singing, all-dancing Adobe Photoshop to free software that was supplied with your camera or scanner. It's tempting to categorise them by cost but this can imply that the cheaper and free software is not worth considering.

I've chosen to highlight some applications you might like to try, but it is a fairly subjective list based on software I've used myself. Let's start with the free stuff.

It's common now for some image editing software to be included with digital cameras, scanners and printers. In fact you usually get two sorts of software with the hardware – there is the essential driver, which controls how the hardware works (there is more about printer drivers in the chapter on Direct Printing) and some extra software which might include an image editing program. These can be very basic but may well include all you need to produce, for example, simple digital negatives.

> *.net is a piece of software. It's a bit like a food mixer - you have a central motor to which you add other devices, like a blender, that all use the same motor. You have to install .net, the motor, before you can install and use paint.net.*

Where the freebies get more interesting is when you get to programs like Paint.net which is free to download and use. Features are being added to this application all the time so it's worth keeping an eye on their web site www.getpaint.net. At the time of writing, there are only a few items missing that I would like to use in textile work. I find it friendly, simple and intuitive to use. It was designed to 'feel' like Photoshop so if you have used any of the Photoshop products you will probably be able to find your way round this one. Just be aware that you will need to download and install the .net environment before you can edit your photos using paint.net.

Another program you might like to consider is called the GIMP (great name). This is also free to download and use from www.gimp.net. As a long term user of Photoshop variations (with varying levels of skill, I have to say!) I found the GIMP harder to get started with. It does, however, have a wealth of features and tools available.

In the mid-price range of software (by this I mean under £100) there are a number of contenders but the two I, personally, like best are Adobe Photoshop Elements and Corel PaintShop Pro. Both are comprehensive and fairly easy to use.

At the professional level there is only really Adobe Photoshop – this will probably do anything you can imagine. However, it is huge, complex and expensive – currently in the region of £600.

For the purposes of illustrating the techniques in this book I've chosen to use Adobe Photoshop Elements – it's a very comprehensive, mid-priced, easy to use piece of software. It's easily available and will do everything discussed in this book.

FILE FORMATS

What are file formats? Well, they are different image file types. Image editing software can read and manipulate only a specified set of different file formats. Each format is identified by a three letter file extension (the bit that comes after the dot) so fred.tif indicates a tiff file and barney.jpg indicates a jpeg file. Some formats like tiffs and jpegs are pretty universal and can be read or opened in most image editing software. Other formats are specific to certain software. Photoshop has its own format, which is identified by the .psd extension. So, wilma.psd is a photoshop specific file. Your image editing software knows how to save a variety of different file formats, holding, if you like, a template for each one. When you come to save an image your software needs to know what format you want it to end up in, so it can apply the right set of instructions. Software like Elements or PaintShop Pro can use many different file formats and can convert easily from one to another

Jpeg stands for Joint Photographic Experts Group – I just put that in because I happen to know. This is a lossy format ie some of the picture information is lost each time the file is saved so the quality is slightly degraded. There are various levels of compression used – the highest level (ie most compression) gives the smallest file size but the lowest quality of image.

Tiff stands for Tagged Image File Format - yes, showing off again! These files on the other hand are termed lossless, ie no information

One of the things I like about Elements is that you can work at several different levels, called modes. Select the mode you want by clicking on the triangle next to Edit Full. The idea is that If you are a complete novice you can use the EDIT Quick Mode which is a set of automatic tools to tidy up or change your images – you say what you want to do and Elements decides how to do it. As you grow in confidence you can use the EDIT Guided mode (akin to a Windows wizard), which will take you step by step through a given process, giving you a range of tools and options but letting you decide. Finally, you have EDIT Full where you have full control and manually select the tools and options you want.

In this book we'll be using the EDIT Full mode throughout as it gives you the full range of options and settings and is pretty straight forward to use. Just take it a bit at a time..

There is a very useful little application called Irfanview, which is free, that will let you open files that you don't have the native application for and convert it to something you can open with your software. So, if someone sends you a file that uses their camera's own file format, you may be able to open it in Irfanview and convert it to a pds (Photoshop) or other format file you can use.

www.irfanview.com

Some digital photography books spend several pages describing the various formats and what they are best used for so if you'd like more information on this I suggest you consult one of them.

My admittedly rather simplistic view is that there are two main things to remember: one is that every time you save a jpeg file, some of the file information is lost and the image is slightly degraded whereas with TIFF or PSD files, none of the file information is lost. The other is that layers are not saved with a jpeg file whereas they are with a tiff file. See the section on layers later in the chapter for why this is so important.

Compression

Graphic files (pictures) are notoriously BIG – they take up a lot of space on your hard disk and can take a long time when they are processed in some way (eg when the size is changed) so over the years methods of compression have been developed which make the file size smaller without, hopefully, reducing the quality of the image too much. This is called compression and refers to how much the size of the file is reduced (the amount of hard disk it takes up), when it's saved.

is discarded when the file is saved. The files are bigger than jpgs.

Digital cameras often give you the option of saving your pictures in different formats - tiff, jpg and raw being the most common. Some also offer the manufacturer's own format but this is usually only readable by the software that comes with the camera. If it's available I save my pictures in tiff format or, failing that, in high resolution jpg. If I've taken a jpg then I would convert it to tiff using File > Save As, selecting TIFF in the dropdown Format list, as soon as I've downloaded it to my computer. All the manipulations then take place on the tiff version and no picture information is discarded.

OVERVIEW OF PHOTOSHOP ELEMENTS

Some useful shortcuts	
Undo	ctrl-Z
Redo	ctrl-Y
Cut	ctrl-X
Copy	ctrl-C
Paste	ctrl-V
Zoom in	ctrl-+
Zoom out	ctrl--

Elements is made up of two separate but interlinked programs, the Organiser and the Editor. The Organiser is where you can view, catalogue and tag your images. Covering the many facilities of this program is beyond the scope of this book but it is worth investigating – try Barbara Brundage's book for a good explanation. If you are not sure which part you are in, and the screens can be a bit confusing to start with, then look at (2) above. This is the button to launch the other part of Elements. So, If it says Organizer then you are in the Editor and if it says Editor then you are in the Organizer.

Here, we'll be concentrating on the Editor where the creative stuff happens. There is only room for a taster of what Elements can do so I've selected the bits I think you need to know for you to be able to develop your skills beyond this book and the techniques I think are most relevant to textile work. I've included my favourite books in the Bibliography.

In the Editor screen there are four main areas you need to be aware of. Across the top (3) is the Menu bar. Click on a menu to see the options available for each one. For instance, as with most Windows applications, the File menu has options such as Open, Save and Print. Many of the options have a keyboard shortcut listed next to them. Ctrl-P (hold the ctrl key down and press P) takes you straight to the Print option. If the option is something you use a lot then it's worth learning what the keyboard shortcut is.

See the screenshot on the previous page.

The next area to look at is the Tool bar (4) down the left hand side of the screen. Hold the cursor over each tool icon to see what the tool is called. For instance the capital T is the text tool. If the tool icon has a triangle in the bottom right corner it means that there are other tools hidden underneath. Hold the left hand button of the mouse down while the cursor is over the tool and the other tools will be visible and available for selection.

NB You have a tool selected at all times so you don't deselect a tool, you simply select a different one.

A linked area is the Options bar (5) at the top of the screen, underneath the menus. Only the options relevant to the selected tool are shown on the Options bar. So, for instance, if the Text tool is selected then you will see options that will let you select the typeface, the size of the text, the colour of the text and so on. If you select the crop tool, as shown opposite, you'll have the option to set the width and height of the area you are going to select for cutting out.

The remaining two areas are the Palette bin (6) and the Project bin (7). A palette is a way to group options that you would probably use together in one place. I usually have two on my screen because I use them a lot - one is the Layers palette that I will explain later in the chapter, and the other is the Undo History. Every time you do something to an image - open it, crop it, draw on it with a brush, create a new layer and so on - then an entry is made in the Undo History. As the name would suggest you can click on any of the entries above the current one and undo them. So it doesn't matter if you make a mistake, even several steps back, you can easily undo it/them.

Be aware that the palettes, bins and tool bar can be minimised or switched off in various ways to make more working space on your monitor - see the Window menu for the options available and the Help system for how to do this.

If you only want to undo the most recent step you can always use the keyboard shortcut for speed - ctrl-Z.

The Project bin is the box at the bottom of the screen where you can see all the images you have open at any given time. You can double click any image in the bin to bring it up into the main editing area.

THE BASICS

I would STRONGLY recommend that you have a copy of Photoshop Elements open when you are reading the next few sections and click on items as I mention them so that you can see what they look like and how they work together. It's difficult to show things moving in a book ...

Rotate

Before you start cropping or re-sizing your image you may want to rotate your image and look at it from different angles. Most imaging software will let you rotate by 90°, or 180° or by a specified number of degrees, clockwise (right) or counter clockwise (left).

If the image is abstract rather than figurative the patterns may be more pleasing at one angle than another. So, have a play and see what you like best.

Image > Rotate

In the Rotate menu options you will see three groups - the top group refers to the whole image, the middle group refers to the selected layer only and the bottom group contains the Straighten tools to correct a faulty horizon line or a leaning building. The options for rotating a layer will become clear later in the chapter. For now, just open an image and try rotating it using the options in the top section.

Crop

Cropping is the term used for cutting out a piece of an image. It's often used to get rid of clutter round the edges to concentrate on the main elements of the image.

The Crop tool works by placing the cursor at the top left hand corner of the section you want to cut out. Then dragging diagonally

For most of the image transfer methods you need to mirror (flip) the image before you print it. The option you need for this is Image > Rotate > Flip Horizontal..

The curse of the disassociated cursor

I blush to tell this tale but I once spent two days trying to work out why, when I tried to crop an image, the cursor, instead of being on the bottom right corner of the crop box, went wandering off on its own. In the end I bought an upgrade to the software, installed it and the problem was fixed only to reappear a few weeks later - gnashing of teeth! There was then one of those "Oh, xxxxxxx" moments. The problem occurred when I had a fixed Aspect Ratio selected and Elements, quite correctly, wouldn't let me draw a crop box that was the wrong shape for the sizes I had specified. Selecting an Aspect Ratio of 'No Restriction' solved the problem. How embarrassing!

If you want to crop a square as opposed to a rectangle then hold the Shift key down while you drag the cursor

down to the bottom right hand corner of your selection using the left hand mouse button. The area outside your selection darkens and each side of the selection will have a drag handle that you can pull in or out to make the selection bigger or smaller. You can also move the selection around by dragging it with the cursor. Click inside the selection and drag it, releasing the mouse when you have it where you want it. You can also move the selection by using the cursor (arrow) keys which move the selection in very small increments to fine tune the position.

Once you have the section you want to keep selected then press the Enter key or click on the green tick at the bottom right of the image.

If you decide you want to cancel the crop then simply press the Esc key or click on the red 'No' sign next to the green tick.

You can also set the specific width and height of the area you want to crop in the Options bar - make sure the Crop tool is selected. Say you want to print on a standard 6" x 4" piece of photo paper. You can type these dimensions in to the relevant boxes. Elements will then only let you crop a piece of the image that is in the right proportions to fit on your paper.

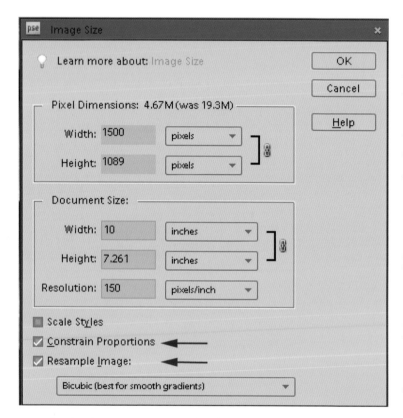

Re-size

Before you print any image you need to specify how big you want your printed image to be. You do this in the Image Size dialogue box - Image > Resize > Image size

The top section of the box refers to the size of the image in pixels.

The bottom section refers to the size of the printed image. It's made up of three parts, the width, the height and the resolution you are going to print at. If you are new to all this then make sure the two boxes at the bottom, Constrain Proportions and Resample Image, are both ticked. Set the resolution to something around 180 and type in either the width or the height. If your image is taller than it is wide (portrait) then type in the height and the width will adjust

accordingly. If your image is wider than it is tall (landscape) then type in the width and let the height adjust itself. Once you are a little more confident then read the section on Resolution on the next pages so you understand how it all works together. You can then make more informed choices.

Before we leave resizing images there are two other things I want to explain.

In the chapter on Direct Printing there is a section on Banner Printing. In order to produce a long thin image ready to print on a banner you either have to distort an image or combine several images into one. To distort the image, deselect Constrain Proportions at the bottom on the Image Size Dialogue box and then put in your chosen width and height. You can achieve some great abstract designs like this.

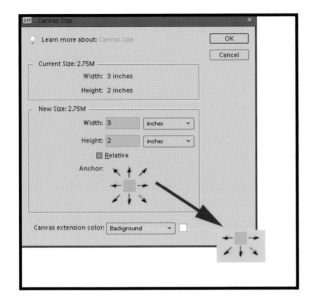

If you want to combine a variety of images together or repeat an image to make a pattern then you will need to know the difference between an image and its canvas. The easiest way to explain this is to think of it as two pieces of fabric - the image is on the front piece and behind is a backing cloth, the canvas. Unless you increase its size you don't see it. To increase the size of the canvas, use

Image > Resize > Canvas Size

In the dialogue box, shown on the top left, you can type in the dimensions you want and you can also specify the direction. If you leave the Anchor box as it is, the extra canvas will be spread evenly around the image, perhaps to indicate a seam allowance. If you want all the new canvas at the bottom of the image, as shown by the white box on the middle image, click on the arrow at the top centre of the Anchor box so that it changes to the one shown by the arrow.

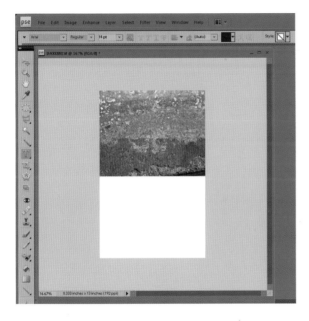

For extra canvas to the left, click on the arrow on the right of the box and so on. Basically, the extra canvas will be in the direction the arrows are pointing, based on the dimensions you specify.

As an example of why you might want to increase the canvas size I used some additional functions, the instructions for which are given later in this chapter. I used the marquee tool to select the original image, copied it on to a new layer, rotated it and dragged it on to the new canvas to make the start of a simple repeating pattern - bottom left.

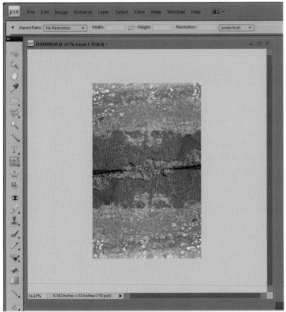

Adding text

To add text to your image, click on the Text tool, the capital T in the tool box, then click on the image where you want to start adding text. Type in the text. Yup, it's that simple.

The font, colour and size of the text can be varied by highlighting it with the mouse first and then changing the settings on the Options bar. The text can also be moved by dragging it with the mouse while the ctrl key is held down.

You can change the shape of the text by, again, highlighting it and then selecting the Create Warp Text button on the Options bar (a T with a curved line underneath). Then select a shape from the Style drop down list - you can

Resolution

I would suggest you don't try and absorb all the information on resolution at one go if you are new to all this - it can be a little daunting. Take a section at a time and understand what it means, then do another one once you've absorbed the first.

* * * * *

Resolution means different things in different contexts. It's like the word 'print' - that can mean something produced using a screen printing method, something produced by a printer connected to a computer or something produced in a darkroom from a photographic negative. They are all sort of 'picture' things but basically are quite different. Resolution is like that, so I'll take each type in turn and explain what it is.

Detail of a digital photograph, enlarged to show individual pixels.

Image resolution:

Digital pictures, whether scanned or taken with a digital camera, are made up of picture elements (pixels) - they are the building blocks of a digital image. Imagine that an image is made up of a grid of tiny squares - each square is a pixel and contains information about the colour and brightness of that part of the image. When the picture is sent to a monitor, to be displayed, or to a printer, then the device converts this digital information into a visual representation of it.

Image resolution simply refers to the number of pixels in an image. A lot of pixels means a high resolution image, a small number means a low resolution image. High resolution images have more detail, less graininess and more subtle transitions of colour and tone.

If you want to get technical then this type of image, made up of pixels, is called a raster image. The other type, a vector image, is formed quite differently, using a mathematical formula.

A mid-range camera, at the time of writing, will capture 10 megapixels, ie the sensor in the camera splits the picture into 10 million pixels, each recording a tiny section of the picture. In any digital camera, taking pictures at its highest resolution setting will split the picture into more pixels than at a lower setting and will capture more information about the picture. This results in a sharper, more detailed picture, especially when it is enlarged.

By the way, the megapixel number in a camera's specification is derived by multiplying the width of the image in pixels by the height of the image in pixels. At its highest resolution my somewhat elderly digital camera produces an image 3456 pixels by 2304 pixels or 8 megapixels.

Monitor resolution:

This refers to the number of pixels that can physically be displayed by the monitor. My main monitor can display a maximum of 1280 x 1024 pixels. As it is approximately 15" wide that works out at roughly 85 pixels per inch (ppi).

Printer resolution

An inkjet printer works by squirting minute droplets of ink onto your paper and part of the specification of the printer is its maximum resolution, usually given in dpi (dots per inch) but each droplet of ink does not equate to a pixel of your image. In fact Tim Daly in his book 'The Digital Printing Handbook' suggests that in order to get a more realistic figure you take the quoted resolution for your printer, eg 1440, and divide it by the number of ink cartridges in the printer eg 4 (cyan, magenta, yellow and black). This gives 360 dpi. This figure is the highest number you should use in the Image Size dialogue box for the resolution you are going to print at as your printer simply cannot print at any higher resolution whatever you feed to it. Increasing the resolution you print at over and above this figure will simply increase the size of the file and will slow down processing and printing speeds.

Likewise, if you look at a printer dialogue box you will usually see several quality options such as 'draft', 'photo' and 'best photo', each of which will use a different printer resolution when you print, ie the printer doesn't always print at its highest capability. For instance Epson quotes 180 dpi for 'draft', 1440 dpi for 'photo' and 2880 dpi for 'best photo' on one of my printers. Again, dividing this number by the number of cartridges in the printer gives an approximation of the print resolution you should set in the Image Size dialogue box.

Print Resolution (as opposed to PrintER resolution)

When you go to Image > Resize > Image size you will see two sets of dimensions. The top box refers to the image size in pixels. The bottom box refers to the Document Size ie the size the document will be when it's printed. This is made up of the width, the height and the print resolution (not the printER resolution).

The resolution you print at will determine how big each pixel of your image will be when it's printed. Say you have a digital image 2200 x 1600 pixels. If you print it at 200 dpi it will produce a print 11" by 8", ie the number of pixels on each side divided by the resolution. If you printed the same file at 300 dpi then the print would be a little over 7" by 5" as each pixel would be squashed into a smaller space when printed.

To see how this works, make a new image - File > New > Blank File - and set the size to 1000 by 500 pixels. Open the Image Size dialogue box - Image > Resize > Image Size and make sure the Resample Images option is off. Taking our image of 1000 pixels by 500 pixels if the print resolution is set to 100 ppi (pixels per inch) then the image will print at 10" x 5". If the resolution is set to 200 ppi then the image will print at 5" x 2.5". THE NUMBER OF PIXELS HASN'T CHANGED BUT THE SIZE OF EACH PIXEL HAS. If the print resolution is low the image will spread out over a greater area and each pixel will be bigger. It follows therefore that if you have a low resolution image (one with a small number of pixels) and you want to print a big version of it then each pixel will be big and the image may look grainy.

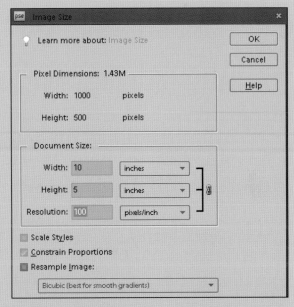

Now click on the Resample box and again change the resolution - this time the dimensions don't change but the number of pixels in the top box does. What is happening is that the software is inserting pixels to make the numbers right. It is guessing - this is called interpolation.

If the Resample option is selected then you have one more setting to fine tune how it works. There is a drop down list at the bottom of the dialogue box with various options. If you are increasing the size of an image then select Bicubic Smoother. If you are decreasing the size of an image then select Bicubic Sharper. I haven't a clue how these work ...

So, to sum up, if you can achieve the dimensions you want to print at a suitable resolution without resampling then that will give you the best quality image. However, as I've said before we are printing on to a broken (woven) surface so we can often use a lower quality image without much detriment. Use your own judgement - do you like the result you've got? If so, go with it - your intent is more important that having the ultimate in 'good' images. Sometimes good enough is good enough.

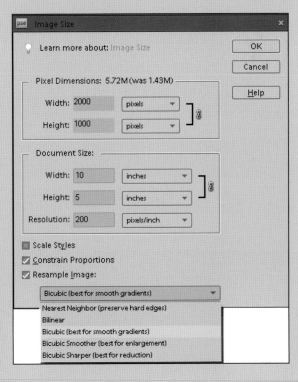

experiment with the sliders to adjust the amount and direction of the selected distortion.

It's very easy to add another text insertion point by mistake when you are trying to highlight the text. If you do, just press the Escape key to get rid of it and try again. You need to have the cursor very close to the text before you start to swipe it. I don't know why but I find it easier to highlight the text backwards, ie right to left rather than left to right.

The other problem is that sometimes you start to type and it doesn't look as though any text is appearing. There are two common reasons for this. Firstly, the text colour, shown in the Options bar, is the same as the background colour - I have tried to type white text on to a white background! The other reason is that you are adding text to a very high resolution image. If you have a small font size on a very big image then the text is VERY small in comparison. If you zoom in to the image - ctrl-+ - several times and the text appears then simply increase the size of the font you are using.

MAKING SELECTIONS AND REMOVING BACKGROUNDS

This section is one of the most important things to understand in Elements. So often you need to select part of your image and then do something to it. For instance if you want to remove a background then you need to be able to select it first. I'm going to start with the basics.

Whatever tools you are going to use to make your selection there are a couple of functions you can use that apply to any selection. Firstly, ctrl-D cancels the selection and you can start again if you get in a twist.

The other thing is that once you have made your selection you can change the size of it by selecting Transform Selection from the Select menu. You can drag any of the handles on the sides to make the selection bigger or smaller and if you hover your cursor just outide one of the corners until you see the curved line appear then you can rotate the selection. These transformations only apply to the selection not to the image. (Not available in versions 6 & 7 of Elements - look in Select > Modify instead).

We'll now look at some specific methods.

To select the whole image, perhaps to copy it on to another image for a collage, click on ctrl A - an easy one to remember, A for All. You'll see what are known as the marching ants marking the boundary of the selection.

Next, we're going to use the rectangular Marquee tool, the dashed rectangle in the Tool bar, to select a section of the image. Position the cursor at the top left hand side of the area you want to select then drag the cursor down to the bottom right of the selection. Like a crop box you can pick the selection up with the mouse and move it or use the cursor keys to move it in small increments.

Holding the ctrl key down turns any tool into the Move tool (see the cursor change when you hold the ctrl key down). So to move a piece of text just hold the ctrl key down and drage the text then release the ctrl key when it's in the right place.

One thing that I think has detracted from the use of digital images in textile work has been the sheer squareness of the images – they have often looked like a photo dumped in the middle of a design so one of the most useful things to learn is how to remove a background so that the squareness disappears.

You can use a variety of techniques to remove a background, depending on the facilities your software offers. The most basic one is to use the eraser tool, and to wipe round the sections you want to keep. You can usually change the size of the rubber in the Options so you can erase a big section at a time where you have got a lot to get rid of and a smaller section at a time when you need more control near the edges of the image you want to keep. Play about with a copy of a picture so you can see what I mean.

You may also like to have a look at the Background Eraser tool - hidden underneath the Eraser tool on the tool bar.- see the Help system for how this works.

*Holding the **Shift** key down while making a selection is the equivalent of selecting the Add to Selection option.*

*Holding the **Alt** key down is the equivalent of selecting the Subtract from Selection option.*

Filling selections with colour.

I've coloured the selections so you can see them more easily.

Right at the bottom of the tool bar you can see two overlapping rectangles. The top left rectangle is called the foreground colour and the bottom right one is the background colour.

I think these terms are misleading as they don't refer to the background or foreground colours of the image but are simply two colours you have available for your tools to use. So, for instance, if you start drawing a line with the Line Tool then it will be in the foreground colour. Or if you use the eraser to remove part of an image it will use the background colour.

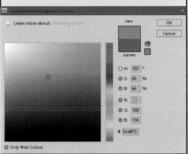

To change the colour of either of these click on the relevant rectangle and select the colour you want to use. Start by clicking on the central bar to select the approximate colour you want, eg green, then select the exact colour by clicking on it in the left hand box and click OK. You can also click on part of your image to 'sample' a colour and allocate it to the foreground or background colours ready to be used.

Alternatively you can enter the hexadecimal (lovely word!) in the bottom box next to the # sign, if you know what it is.

In order to fill a selection you use:

Alt-backspace *to fill with the foreground colour.*

Ctrl-backspace *to fill with the background colour..*

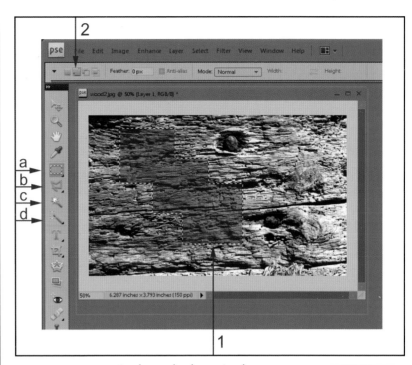

a - marquee tools   b - lasso tools

c - magic wand   d - quick selection tool

If you are using any of the tools that can make a selection then you will notice a set of four icons on the left hand side of the Options bar - these are VERY useful. You will need to use the middle two for a number of the techniques in this book. I would suggest that you practise using them with the marquee tools so you can see

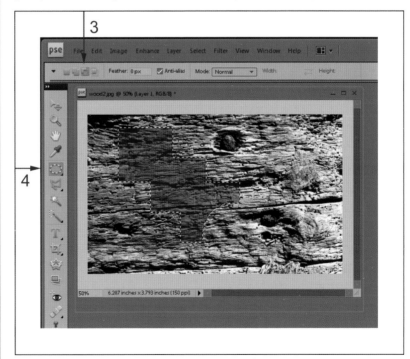

their effects easily. The second from the left is Add to Selection (2 - above. Say you have selected a rectangle and want to add on another section then click on the Add to Selection icon before you draw the second rectangle.

The third icon from the left (3) is Subtract from Selection. This does just what it says. If you click on Subtract from Selection then the next shape you draw or select will be taken away from the main selection. Just to show the principle, I've used the elliptical marquee tool to take a circular bite out of the selection on the bottom right hand corner. This works in the same way as the rectangle marquee tool by dragging from the top left to the bottom right. Holding the Shift key down while you are dragging will give you a circle rather than an ellipse.

I know this example is rather simplistic but it shows the principle of making a selection in several steps, adding and taking away areas as you work. It is very rarely that you can make a meaningful selection in one step.

Another general set of selection tools are the lasso tools (yeeha! - sorry couldn't resist!). The most useful one for me is the polygonal lasso tool. Select the tool - under the marquee tools in the Tool bar - then click where you want to start your selection. Move the cursor to the next point on the boundary of your shape and click again. Continue moving and clicking until you have got back to the start of your selection. Click on the start point and you should see the marching ants.

This tool is great for selecting closed shapes and, if you take it in small steps, it can cope with curved shapes as well as geometric ones.

Now for a couple of more sophisticated selection tools - these are the two I use most in my own work.

The **Magic Wand Tool** selects pixels of the same or similar colour. There are two options on the Options bar that you need to consider particularly - the first is the Contiguous tick box. If the Contiguous box is ticked then only pixels next to each other will be selected, as in the left hand picture below. If you untick this box then all pixels of the same or similar colour anywhere in the image will be selected, as in the right hand image.

The other option that makes a big difference is the Tolerance setting in the Options bar. This controls how much leeway you give the software. If the Tolerance setting is very low then you are telling the software that you only want to select pixels that are very close in colour to the one you click on. If the tolerance setting is high then you are saying that you want to select pixels that are more or less like the one you've clicked.

 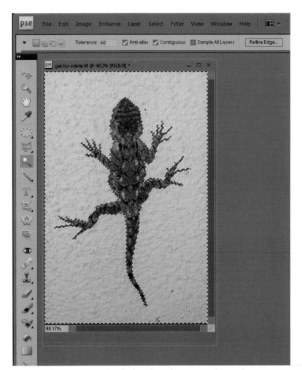

In this image of George the gecko, last seen in Peru, I wanted to get rid of the background so that I could make a thermofax screen from him. Since the background is fairly uniform I can use the Magic Wand tool. In the left hand image the Tolerance is low (20) and Contiguous, meaning 'next to', is off so only part of the background is selected and some of the pattern on George's back is selected. By increasing the Tolerance to 60 and switching the Contiguous setting on I can select all the background and none of George, as in the right hand image, since none of the pixels on his back are 'next to' the ones selected.

Once I have the background selected then I can press the Delete key and I will have just George with no rectangular block around him.

The next tool to have a look at is the **Quick Selection** tool which is brilliant. Whereas the Magic Wand looks for pixels of colour, this tool looks for edges.

In this picture of a lily I wanted to get rid of the background so I would end up with just the main lily head. As the background is busy and complicated I decided to work on the lily head itself. By dragging the cursor down the centre of a petal the Quick Selection tool tried to find the edges of the petals.

Original photographs: Tony Booth

Working an area at a time, and making sure the Add to Selection option is selected, I achieved a rough-cut of the flower head. Then alternating between the Subtract from Selection and Add to Selection options I tidied up the edges.

The tool will have trouble sometimes deciding where an edge is. The human brain is very good at discerning shapes by using its experience. For instance, at the top right hand side of the lily head there is the edge of a white petal next to a white flower. We know there's an edge there even though there is virtually no difference in colour but the software is logical and sometimes has problems. I

tend to use the Quick Selection tool to get a rough cut of the image and then tidy it up manually later. It often helps to smooth out the edges of a selection to click on the aptly named 'Refine Edge' option. This attempts to take out any lumps and bumps in the curves and usually does a pretty good job.

Once the lily head is selected, invert the selection so that the background is selected - Select > Inverse - and delete it to give the lily head on its own.

Although this will be covered later in the chapter, just be aware that in order to get a transparent background, which is shown in Elements as a chequerboard pattern, the Background layer needs to be unlocked - double click on the layer in the Layers palette and click on OK.

LAYERS BASICS

Layers in Elements act as a series of sophisticated sheets of glass or transparency film. Each layer can contain different images, text, etc. For instance you might want to add some text to a digital photo. Text always appears on a separate layer so you can move it around until it is exactly where you want it.

Layers can be added or removed, lightened or darkened, combined in groups or left separate. They can be moved around in relation to one another. You can rub away part of a layer so you can see the layer underneath and so much more …. I can only give you a quick overview of layers here but I hope I will be able to show you that they are worth spending some time on.

As with most Windows programs there are many different ways to do any given action but I think it makes most sense to use the palettes most of the time. So the instructions I'm going to give you will be a mixture of this with a few keyboard shortcuts thrown in. Just be aware that you can also use the Layers menu at the top of the screen.

The layers palette, usually on the right hand side of your screen, is the control centre for your stack. If you can't see a Layers Palette go to the Windows menu, click on Layers and the palette should appear. You can either leave it floating, so you can move it around, or you can dock it with the other palettes in the palette bin.

When you open a photograph the image automatically becomes the background layer. This does not refer to the background of the image but to the fact that it is the base layer at the bottom of the layer stack. Notice that there is a padlock symbol on the layer. Unless you unlock it the background layer will always be at the bottom of the stack and you can't make any part of it transparent. Transparency is shown on your screen by a chequerboard effect.

To unlock the background layer, double click on it in the Layers palette. In the dialog box that comes up you can give the layer a new name, if you wish, or you can simply click on OK. The layer is then unlocked and the padlock symbol will have disappeared.

NB – if you want to save the layers with the image so that you can go back and work on them

individually later on, you must save the image in .tif, .pds or sometimes .pdf format. Jpegs don't retain their layer information when saved.

In order to get the idea of how layers work I suggest you do the following exercise, watching the changes in the Layer palette at each stage. Consult the chart on the next page to see how to do each step or if you need a quick reminder of how to do anything.

Exercise:
NB The active layer is the one you are currently working on - this is shown in the Layers palette in a different colour from the rest. In the example opposite it is the top layer of the two. If something doesn't work as you expect the first thing to check is that you have the right layer active.

➤ Open an image

➤ Add two separate pieces of text in different colours. When you add text Elements automatically makes a new layer for you so you don't have to manually do it first.

➤ Add a new layer between the image and the text – add some brushwork. Select the Brush tool - remember you can move the cursor over the Tool bar to see the names until you find the right one - then doodle on your new layer. You can change the shape and size of the brush by editing the options on the Options bar. You can change the colour you are using by selecting a different foreground colour.

➤ Select both layers of text and link them together – now if you move one the other will move at the same time.

➤ Change the order of the layers and observe the difference.

➤ Delete a layer.

➤ Redo the layer - ctrl-Z.

➤ Change the opacity of one of the layers by clicking on the black triangle next to the Opacity box (4) and moving the slider with the mouse. Observe the changes.

➤ Lock a layer and then try to rub out part of it with the eraser.

Create a new layer	Click on the new layer symbol in the palette (1). This creates a new layer above the active layer. To create a new layer below the active layer, hold the ctrl key down and click on the new layer icon.
Delete a layer	Drag the layer to be deleted to the trash can (3).
Switch off a layer	Click on the eye symbol next to the layer you want to switch off. This doesn't delete the layer, it just makes it temporarily invisible. Switch it back on by clicking the eye icon again.
Move a layer within the stack.	Drag and drop with the mouse. Remember that the background layer has to be unlocked before it can be anywhere but the bottom of the stack.
Create an adjustment layer	Click on the adjustment layer icon (2), and select the type of adjustment you want to make. Adjustment layers do the same jobs as a number of other features. For instance you can change the Brightness/Contrast of an image by selecting Enhance > Adjust Lighting > Brightness/Contrast and adjusting the relevant sliders. Or, you can add a Brightness/Contrast adjustment layer to your image. Adjustment layers affect ALL the layers below them. To apply an adjustment layer ONLY to one layer select 'Create a Clipping Mask' from the Layer menu - in versions 6 and 7 of Elements this was called 'Group with Previous' (ungroup to reverse). This is only available from the Layer menu, NOT the layer palette. Adjustment layers have the advantage that you can go back to the layer at any time and change the settings or you can mover the layer within the pack so that it affects different layers of your image. The best way to understand this is to try some out and observe the changes.
Copy a layer.	Right click on the layer you want to copy and select Duplicate layer. Give the layer a suitable name and click OK.
Lock a layer	To lock the whole layer, click on the padlock next to the word 'Lock' at the bottom of the Layers palette (4) - at the top of the palette in version 6 and 7. You can't then accidentally change something on this layer. To unlock the layer click on the padlock again. To lock ONLY the transparent pixels, click on the chequerboard next to the word 'Lock' and click it again to unlock.
Link layers together, so that they move at the same time	Select the layers you want to link in the Layers palette - ctrl-click on each layer to select multiple individual layers - click on the first layer and shift-click on the last layer to select a group of layers which are next to each other in the stack. Once you have the required layers selected, click on the chain symbol at the bottom of the palette to lock them together. To unlock the layers, select one of the linked layers and click on the chain symbol again.

The Healing Brush may be hidden under the Spot Healing Brush in the tool bar. So, click and hold down the mouse button to see the hidden tools, then select the one you want to use.

As a child at school I was told I couldn't draw and although I learned MUCH later, I still have a hangup about it and am much comfier using a computer. This small section is therefore dedicated to the drawing-phobic.

CLEAN AND REPAIR

I used to use the Clone tool (looks like an old style stamp in the Tool bar) to repair or alter photographs. The most well known use is to repair old photographs by getting rid of scratches etc but it can also be used to erase elements of a photograph you don't want such as obtrusive electricity pylons.

However, Elements has a better tool for this now called the Healing Brush, next to the red eye in the Tool bar. This works in two steps: you alt-click on an area in the image that you want to select replacement pixels from and then swipe on the area of the image you want to repair. You repeat this procedure until you've achieved the result you want.

I find it's best to do this in small steps - sample a bit, repair a bit, sample another bit, repair another bit ... These grapes were scanned and although I liked the result there were specks of something on the dark background so I used the healing brush to get rid of them.

The main difference between this and the older Clone Tool is that the Healing brush tries to blend the new piece into the surrounding area and usually does a good job.

SIMPLIFYING IMAGES

So, why would you want to simplify an image? Embroiderers might want to use a photograph as the basis for a piece of work but find the continuous tones of a photo too complex. Image editing software can reduce the number of colours.

Screenprinters might need to convert an image into balck and white in order to create a photoemulsion or thermofax screen. Designers might want to abstract or take a different view of an image.

You can simplify an image in terms of its colours or in terms of its outlines or both. We'll look at each one separately.

Simplifying colours

Posterizing reduces the number of colours in an image so you end up with a series of more abrupt changes of colour rather than a smooth transition. You'll find it under the Filters menu in adjustments. Select the number of levels you want and click on OK. You can then print on to aida or calico as detailed in the chapter on Direct Printing.

Original photograph

Posterized photograph

Creating black and white images from a colour photo

Several techniques such as screen printing require a black and white image rather than a continuous tone one. After all, each little piece of the screen printing mesh is either open to let ink through or closed - it can't be a 'bit' open.

There are many ways to do this but they won't all work well on all photographs. So, if you don't like the result from one method, try another.

First of all you could try converting the image to greyscale, using the 'Convert to Black and White' option in the Enhance menu. This is a bit of a misnomer as it produces a greyscale image, ie it has tones of grey as opposed to a black and white image which has only pure black and pure white.

Original Photograph: Carol Hampton

Converted to greyscale using the Infrared style

This is a really nice tool - you have the before and after views of the image at the top with a series of pre-set styles underneath. These give different versions of the greyscale image using differing amounts of red, green and blue. Open an image and click on each style in turn to see the effects of each. Usually one will please you more than the others so leave that one selected. You can fine tune if you wish by using the individual colour channel sliders. Just try moving each one and observe the effect.

You also have a Contrast slider - moving it to the right increases the contrast, to the left decreases it.

Method 1 - Threshold Filter
Once you have your greyscale image you can then try applying a threshold filter. This converts your greyscale image to black and white. Filter > Adjustments > Threshold

Move the slider along until you like the effect best. This gives a bold, striking result.

Threshold filter applied

Trace Contours applied

Original photograph: Tony Booth

Glowing Edges applied

Image inverted

Threshold applied

Method 2 - Trace Contours

The next method gives a very different result. The process starts the same way by converting the image to greyscale but you then apply a different filter.

Filter > Stylize > Trace Contour

As you can see, this gives a very light result in the style of a sketch.

Method 3 - Glowing Edges

As is often the way, I came across this combination of a filter and two adjustment layers while I was trying to do something completely different! If you are not sure what adjustment layers are then look back to the Layers Basics section in this chapter.

Open the image you want to convert then apply the Glowing Edges filter - Filter > Stylize > Glowing Edges

Add a new adjustment layer from the Layer palette to invert the image - New Adjustment layer > Invert

Then add a second New Adjustment layer to give a black and white image - New Adjustment layer > Threshold – move the slider to the right until you like the result.

I think this is the place to give my 'follow the recipe' talk. Basically, with something like image editing you would have to spend a lot of time and study to be able to understand exactly how everything works but a lot of the time it is enough to know that it does. If you can follow a 'recipe' and get the results you want, does it matter that you don't understand exactly how each step works? After all if you are making bread you may not understand the chemistry of how yeast produces bubbles to expand the dough, you just know that it does.

It's certainly true with IT that the more you understand, you more options you have and the more likely you are to be able to sort out something that is going wrong, but you can achieve an awful lot while you are learning.

Method 4 - Black & White Recipe

The next method I'm going to describe is adapted from part of a recipe in John Beardsworth's book, Photoshop Fine Art Cookbook for Digital Photographers (details in Bibliography - a 'must get' if you like this sort of thing). He uses this as the first step to producing Pop Art images. I was familiar with most of the steps in the recipe but a couple of his steps in the middle turned out to be the 'missing link' that on some images makes all the difference. The sequence goes something like this:

➤ Open the image and double click on the background layer to unlock it. You can give it a new name if you wish - perhaps Original.

➤ Right click on this layer and select Duplicate Layer. Name the new layer Blurry.

➤ With the Blurry layer active, set the blending mode to 'Colour dodge' – this is at the tope of the Layers palette. Click on the black triangle next to the word Normal and select Colour Dodge from the drop down list.

➤ Next invert the image to give a negative - Filter > Adjustments > Invert. Don't panic at this stage - quite often the image disappears altogether which can be a bit disconcerting. Just carry on to the next stage.

➤ Apply a gaussian blur - Filter > Blur > Gaussian blur – use the slider in the Radius box at the bottom to control the line width. Generally a low setting here will give the best results - try one or two pixels to start with.

➤ Add a new adjustment layer from the Layer palette to apply the threshold filter - New adjustment layer > Threshold – use the slider until you have as much detail showing as you want.

If you don't like the end result it sometimes helps to go back to the gaussian blur step, using the Undo History, and repeat the blur with a different radius.

Method 5 - Halftone

The last method I'm going to describe in this section is to do with the halftone filter. This filter splits the image into small squares and fills each square with a circle the size of which relates to the brightness of that part of the image. So a bright area will have small circles and a dark area will have bigger circles. This simulates the look of old newspaper pictures.

➤ Open the image you want to convert

➤ Apply the halftone filter - Filter > Sketch > Halftone. Here I've used a Size of 6 and I've increased the Contrast to 50.

➤ Finally, apply a threshold filter either from the Filter menu - Filter > Adjustments > Threshold - or as an adjustment layer. Move the slider until you get the result you like best.

I rather like the somewhat exaggerated dottiness here but if you want a more refined image, use a smaller number for the size setting.

There is another halftone filter - Filter > Pixelate > Color Halftone. To use this for our purposes here, convert the image to greyscale first, then apply the filter. As the image is greyscale you only have two settings to adjust, the Maximum Radius and Channel 1. The other three channels refer to colour images. A bigger value in Maximum Radius will give a coarser image.

Finally, apply a threshold filter either from the Filter menu - Filter > Adjustments > Threshold - or as an adjustment layer. Move the slider until you get the result you like best.

A proper description of blending modes is way outside the scope of this book - I have an entire book written on just this subject! - and I'm not sure I could do it anyway! I do find them difficult to understand, but that doesn't stop me using them. In simple terms a blending mode controls how the contents of selected layers are blended together to give a composite of some sort.

There will be more uses of them later in this chapter when we look at Edges and Borders.

Pictures opposite show the original photograph, taken by Robert Hewson, which was converted to black and white using method 4. I then printed this on to hand dyed silk using an inkjet printer and pigment-based ink.

EDGES AND BORDERS

You sometimes want to add a border or decorative edge to your images. There are many ways to do this - I've picked out four that I think you might like.

Soft edge

Select the brush tool (1) and select a soft edged style from the drop down list (2) - hover your mouse over the options to see what they are called - and a suitable size (3) from the Options bar at the top of the screen

Make sure the colour you want for your soft edge is selected as the foreground colour (4). If you want this image to blend into another background image, perhaps as part of a collage, you might want to sample the base image and set that as the foreground colour.

Holding the Shift key down, to ensure your strokes are straight and parallel to the sides, stroke each edge of the image with the brush.

Of course, you don't have to reflect the original rectangular shape of the image when you are softening the edges. You can paint round the edges in any shape you like.

This one's for Barbara!

Snowdrops showing two sides softened with a 300 pixel soft brush using white as the foreground colour.

Or you could use the eraser tool, set to a softbrush or airbrush setting and erase sections of the image to reflect the shape of a particular element. If you are working on the background layer and it is locked then the soft edges will be the foreground colour. If the layer is unlocked then the soft edges will be transparent.

Things do get a little more complicated when you have an image with multiple layers as the eraser will only rub out on the active layer.

Vignette

This gives that traditional faded out effect that is commonly found on old photographs.

➤ Use the elliptical marquee tool with a feather (see the Options bar) set to something like 150, to select part of the image.

➤ Then use Select > Inverse to select the background.

➤ Make a new layer and fill the selection with the background colour (ctrl + backspace) – this can, of course, be sampled from the image if you wish.

➤ At this stage you can either apply a filter to give some texture or you can apply a blending mode from the drop down list at the top of the Layers palette – for this one I simply reduced the opacity a little on the top layer so that some of the original image shows through.

You can use this technique with other selection methods – consider using the lasso tool or the quick selection tool.

Feathering gives a soft edge to a selection. If you are cutting an image out that you want to place on a different one then a feather of a couple of pixels will make the combined image look more natural.

Here we are using a big feather to give the vignette effect.

The star of
our show!

Multi-coloured border

This method uses several techniques we've already covered.

➤ First of all unlock the background layer.

➤ Increase the canvas size of the image by a small amount - Image > Resize > Canvas Size. Up to now we've increased canvas size by a specific amount - this time try selecting Percent from the drop down list of units for the width and height and type in 105 into both the size boxes.

➤ Add a new layer underneath the image layer - ctrl-new layer, from the Layers palette.

➤ Fill this layer with your chosen colour. You can repeat this process several times if you wish, making the canvas a bit bigger each time, to give a multi-coloured border.

By unlocking the layer first the extra canvas is transparent, rather than white, so the new coloured layer below shows through.

See the example on the next page.

Original photograph:

Lesley Houghton

with multi-coloured border

Textured border

Lastly, let's look at how to create a textured border.

> ➤ Open an image (the image)
> ➤ Open a second image (the texture).
> ➤ Make sure both images are the same size - crop or resize if necessary.
> ➤ Copy the texture image - ctrl-A then ctrl-C and paste it on to the main image - ctrl-V. It should be on a separate layer above the main image.
> ➤ Using the rectangular marquee tool select the centre of the texture layer. I like to use a feather of around 100 to give a softer transition between the two images when they are blended together. Delete the selected area. You should now see the image layer in the centre and the texture layer around the edges.

Ctrl-D will get rid of the marching ants once you've deleted the middle.

> ➤ Use a blending mode to blend the two layers together. Ones

Original photograph:

Craig Burton

with textured border

to start with could be Hard Light - used here - Difference, Multiply, Color Dodge and Overlay. It's worth trying a variety of modes as each one will give a different effect depending on the qualities of the two images used.

CREATING DIGITAL POSITIVES AND NEGATIVES

I've already explained several methods for creating black and white images - this section is about producing digital positives and negatives, ie tonal images with shades of grey. These are most often used with photographic style methods such as cyanotypes (blueprints) or inkodye prints.

As usual the instructions here are specific to Adobe Photoshop Elements 8 and assume you are in EDIT Full mode – if you use different software, use the help system or manual to find out where the equivalent options are.

You may wish to start by cropping your image and cleaning up any imperfections using the Healing Brush. After that there are six basic steps to producing a digital negative for our purposes, two of them being optional.

Convert to Greyscale

If your image is in colour, start by coverting it to black and white, or more accurately to greyscale. This takes the colour away and you can then see if the image will 'work' in shades of grey. Some glorious pictures look dull in greyscale as the tones are too close together.

There are a number of ways to do this in Elements but I would start by using the 'Convert to Black and White' option in the Enhance menu.

Enhance > Convert to black and white.

Other methods you might want to consider are de-saturating the image - Enhance > Adjust Color > Adjust Hue/Saturation. Move the Saturation slider all the way to the left. You can do the same thing with an adjustment layer.

If you want more information on the various options for this instruction have a look in the Help or, better, read the section in Barbara Brundage's book on Removing and Adding colour.

Re-size

The next thing is to make the image the right size to fit on the transparency film you are going to use.

All the processes in this book that use digital negatives produce contact prints, so the end result is the same size as the negative.

Image > Resize > Image Size

Adjust contrast (Optional)

After the dimensions are set then you will probably want to increase the contrast of the image. Most of the processes we are going to use negatives with tend to decrease the contrast of the image so by increasing the contrast of the negative the end result should be about right.

Again there are several ways to do this, each with varying degrees of flexibility. The first uses Enhance > Adjust Lighting > Brightness/Contrast

You will see two sliders, the top one controlling the brightness of the image and the bottom one controlling the contrast. Simply drag the bottom slider along to the right a little to increase the contrast. The slight drawback to this is that the change is applied to the whole image whereas you might only want to brighten the highlights and leave the shadows as they are. To do this more conrolled change you need something called curves. Enhance > Adjust Color > Adjust Color Curves.

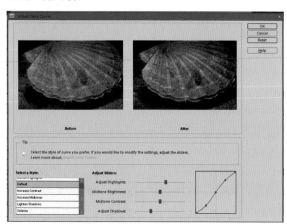

This tool has useful before and after views of your image but it doesn't have the flexibility of the same tool in the full version of Photoshop. You are limited here to either using one of the preset styles on the left or moving the sliders on the right. Try moving the Adjust Highlights slider a little to the right - to brighten the highlights and the Adjust Shadows slider a little to the

Original photograph: Lesley Houghton

I cut the flower head out of Lesley's photograph using the Quick Selection tool with Refine Edges, converted it to greyscale and then lightened the image a little to bring out the lovely texture in the petals. I increased the contrast and sharpened the image a little. This gave me the positive image.

Finally, I inverted the image to give me the negative.

You can see both the positive and the negative of this image printed in the section on Cyanotypes earlier in the book.

You may like to investigate the use of Levels - Enhance > Adjust Lighting > Levels. See the Help system or a manual for what this does and how to use it.

You may also like to try the type of transparency film that is coated with tiny ceramic particles such as PermaJet Digital Transfer Film.

The coating is designed to hold more ink than standard transparency film and should give a better quality negative. These are more expensive than the standard films and, when printing on fabric, I couldn't see much difference

left - to darken the shadows. This approximates the soft 'S' curve traditionally used for digital negatives printed on an inkjet printer.

Adjust sharpness (Optional)

You may want to consider sharpening your image at this point to try and reduce slight blurriness from various causes. A discussion of what this is and how it works is outside the scope of this book but to get you started, have a look at Enhance > Adjust Sharpness or the Unsharp Mask – yes, I agree, not exactly an intuitive name! The main thing is not to over sharpen - if you start getting halos round parts of the image or strange textures then you've probably over sharpened. Undo the last action and try again with lower settings.

At this point you have a Digital Positive and can skip the next section if you wish and go on to printing.

Invert

Invert the image – this reverses the blacks and whites to give a negative. In Elements this is found at Filter > Adjustments > Invert or you can use an adjustment layer. If you can't find this option in your image editing software it might be included in the options on your printer driver dialogue box – look for something like 'print as negative' or 'print inverted'.

Print

Make sure you have the right sort of transparency film for your printer – inkjet transparencies for inkjet printers and laser transparencies for a laser printer. Don't mix up the two. If you use laser transparencies in an inkjet printer the ink will probably smudge but if you put inkjet transparencies in a laser printer they will probably melt!

Some printers have a transparency setting in the printer dialogue box but that probably isn't the best choice. I used the plain paper setting for quite a while but after more experimentation found that I got a better quality negative by using the Glossy Film setting. You may have to do some testing on your own printer to find the best combination.

If you run out of transparency film you can print your negative on to thin paper, let it dry thoroughly, and then oil it lightly on the back to make it translucent. The exposure time for paper negatives will be something like 50% longer than one on transparency film. However, there is a good reason why you might consider one. Many inkjet printers have a facility to print on to a roll of paper so you could make a single negative several feet long using the banner setting ...

Note:

If you are adding text to a negative or a positive then you DON'T need to mirror the text – it will read true.

MORE LAYERS

Layer mask

Adjustment layers each have a layer mask that controls which parts of your image are affected by the adjustment. It's probably easiest to explain what this is and does with an example ...

Open your chosen image and duplicate the background layer.

Create a Hue/Saturation adjustment layer and move the Saturation slider all the way to the left to create a greyscale image.

Now, with the adjustment layer active select the Brush tool with black as the foreground colour and start painting on the image - you can think of this as rubbing out parts of the adjustment layer so that the original version of the image shows through. If you paint on too much you can change to white and reinstate some of the adjustment. You can see in this illustration the shape of the hole in the adjustment on the mask of that layer (1). The end result is that the adjustment is only applied to the areas around the butterfly.

You don't have to use the brush to apply black to the mask, you can use any combination of selection tools to make a selection which you then fill with black.

Clipping path

A clipping path crops an image to the shape of another image underneath it.

Original photograph

Big text

➤ Open your chosen image.

➤ Add some text in a bold font and big size.

➤ Unlock the background layer and pull it to the top of the layer stack, ie so the layer containing the image is above the layer with the text.

➤ Make the top layer active by clicking on it.

➤ From the Layer menu select – Create a clipping path. You can't select this from the Layers palette, only from the menu. In versions 6 and 7 of Elements, this is called Group with Previous.

See the result of this, and the continuation of this section, on page 118.

Examples using layers

This page shows a simple image cut out of a digital photograph and then repeated at different sizes. Each element is on a separate layer.

Each element has had an adjustment layer applied, gradually reducing the saturation of the colours, until the top element is completely de-saturated.

Since I only wanted to apply each adjustment to one layer I grouped it with its layer, otherwise it would have been applied to all the layers below it.

Original photograph:

Barbara Hill

I thought you might like to see how the cover for this book was developed.

I put each image on to a separate named layer so that I could move them round and rotate each one until I achieved the effect I was looking for. Each piece of text automatically went on to a new layer.

GRASSES AND LEAVES

If you are new to all this I would stop here and absorb what you've just done. Then, when you are feeling more adventurous, try the next section.

I then wondered if I could get the grasses and leaves to look as if they were growing through the cut out text.

I copied the original image and pasted it on to a layer at the bottom of the stack. Immediately above it I inserted a new Invert adjustment layer which gave me some nice subtle greyish pink tones. Finally, with the Invert layer active I applied an Exclusion blending mode and got the result below.

FILTERS

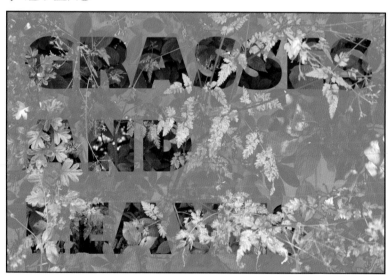

Filters are a nice, light hearted way to change your picture. I believe there are something like 100 filters in Elements so I'm going to leave you to experiment with most of them yourself.

Open an image and then go to the Filter menu, select a category and then a filter eg Filter > Pixelate > Mosaic. This is one that is useful if you want to convert an image for a cross stitch pattern.

Depending on which filter you select, you may get a dialogue box with the relevant options or you may go into the main Filters screen where you can select filters and set options.

You might find it useful to open the Effects palette from the

Window menu. You can then see a visual representation of each filter. Remember that you need to select the category from the drop down list and then select a filter. You need to click on Apply before you can see the results. You'll then see an expanded section of your image with the filter applied, at which point you can either click on OK to accept the filter or Cancel to reject it and try something else.

PLUG-INS

Lastly in this chapter I just want to mention plug-ins. These are additional tools, functions etc that can be downloaded from the Internet and installed in Photoshop Elements. Many are for the full Photoshop program but as Elements is based on this they will mostly work in Elements also. A lot of plug-ins are free, some you have to pay for. Just Google 'Photoshop Elements Plugins' and you'll find more than you know what to do with. Each plugin should come with its own installation instructions - just follow these carefully.

Three sites that I think are worthy of mention are:

www.thepluginsite.com
www.ononesoftware.com
www.mehdiplugins.com - I particularly like the Mehdi Kaleidoscope plug-in which, with two clicks and a drag, will convert the image above into the one on the right. There are numerous settings that you can play with to give a huge range of variations. Oh, and it's free!

Artists' Biographies ...

LESLIE BRANKIN

Lesley Brankin is a textile artist, freelance needlecraft writer and designer living and working in Malvern, Worcestershire. A recipient of many major needlework and quilting awards, at both a national and international level, she has gained a solid reputation for her innovative design work and desire to support others in achieving their full potential. Over the years Lesley has designed and written numerous projects and articles for many of the top UK needlecraft and patchwork magazines and, for 5 years, was an Assistant Editor of British Patchwork & Quilting magazine. She now undertakes work on behalf of several prominent UK product suppliers, including Janome UK Ltd. and has developed her own range of patterns and books.

Having gained a first class joint honours degree in Physical Geography and Geology, Lesley formerly worked in the Oil Industry where she was involved in the early development of computer mapping and visualisation software techniques. Following the completion of a City & Guilds Embroidery and Design course and the birth of her two children, she 'moved' into textiles. Given her background in computing it was natural for her to consider computer graphic techniques as an integral part of her toolbox.

Lesley's recent personal work explores patchwork and quilting as a medium for contemporary textile art. Her work features both paint and computer based print techniques which she combines to create her distinctive 'painterly' style of wholecloth quilts. Some of the paint techniques she uses are described in her latest booklet entitled 'Monoprinting for Quilting'.

To view more examples of Lesley's work visit www.lesleybrankinquilts.co.uk

ROSEMARY F C COUSINS

After leaving School Rosemary went to the Royal School of Needlework, first as a YTS trainee, and then as an apprentice, whilst it was still at Princes Gate. She then went to work with furnishing fabrics before returning to the London College of Fashion to study Fashion Design and Technology.

Her work life then revolved around tailoring and alterations, starting at Savile Row and, after her marriage, at various tailors' shops working her way up the country as her husband's work brought moves from the South Coast to the Midlands and currently to the East Riding of Yorkshire.

At the time she returned to college Rosemary also joined Sir Thomas Blackwell's Regiment of Foot, a re-enactment group of 'The Kings Army' of the 'English Civil War Society'. This enhanced and encouraged her interest in period embroidery and costume techniques and styles.

After the birth of her daughter, she joined the Embroiderers' Guild – Hull & East Riding Branch, which was a great springboard to again try a range of different embroidery techniques, sometimes teaching them. She also started looking again at patchwork and quilting and through that interest went to quilt shows where she met Ruth, and subsequently encouraged her to join HERBs.

Rosemary joined the technology age with a digital camera at Christmas 2007, and a gifted 2nd hand laptop the following autumn. Six months later came the printer an Epson SX205.

Her continuing fascinations include 17th century embroidery and costumes, tailoring, clothing for today for the short and rounded figure, and how to fit it, piecing, patchwork and quilting, and trying not to lose great ideas of things to do, that she now has stored on her computer.

JANE THOMAS

Jane originally trained to teach Textiles at Battersea College of Education in 1974-77 where she was a student of Rozanne Hawksley. She has taught dressmaking in schools and adult education and now works in Learning Support. She embroiders for pleasure!

CATHY CORBISHLEY MICHEL

Cathy came to the first summer school I taught at Missenden Abbey to learn the cyanotype process and how to use digital images on fabric. She worked with the cyanotype methods and took them to another level. Her cyanotype based quilts are beautiful and can be seen at http://www.michelg.plus.com.

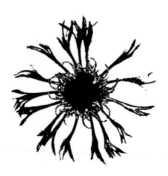

Appendix 1 - Health & Safety ...

You should always read any health and safety recommendations that come with a particular product. It is your responsibility to ensure your own safety. The following guidelines are designed to help you work safely but are not a substitute for your own risk assessment and general common sense.

General good practice

➤ Keep all chemicals away from places where children and animals could come into contact with them or where you store and prepare food.

➤ Don't put your liquid working chemicals into bottles that have been used for drinks to avoid the risk of people mistaking them for soft drinks (many serious cases of poisoning have happened like this).

➤ Keep powders in containers with secure lids and label every container with details of exactly what it contains.

➤ Don't rub your eyes with your hands or gloves after handling chemicals; always wash them thoroughly before you do anything else.

➤ Don't contaminate the inside of gloves or other protective clothing with chemicals as this can cause problems with prolonged contact.

➤ Don't pour chemicals into rivers or streams to avoid harming wildlife.

➤ Don't leave contaminated wet clothes in contact with the skin to avoid creating irritating effects.

➤ Don't eat, drink or smoke when handling chemicals so as to avoid getting them in your mouth.

➤ Do cover work surfaces with newspaper or other absorbent material to soak up spillages – it's easy just to gather contaminated paper together and dispose of it.

➤ Do work in a draught free area to avoid powders etc blowing about and contaminating other surfaces.

Solvents including Acetone and Citra Solv

General guidelines for working with any solvents are:

➤ Use in a well ventilated area or outside. If you are only using tiny quantities then positioning a fan behind you, pointing to an open window may be enough.

➤ Don't breathe in the vapour - it can irritate your respiratory tract. If your work space isn't well ventilated wear a suitable respirator.

➤ Avoid contact with your skin - wear suitable gloves. Generally nitrile gloves are more resistant to solvents than latex ones.

➤ Avoid contact with your eyes - follow the guidance on the Material Safety Data Sheet (MSDS) sheet for the produce.

- ➤ Don't swallow the solvent - I have no idea why you would want to but there are some strange people out there! Seriously though, most solvents could be mistaken visually for a drink so keep them out of the reach of children and pets in their original, well labelled bottles.
- ➤ Replace the lid on the container as soon as you have used it.
- ➤ Keep away from naked flames or other sources of heat - if you have a spillage then don't do anything that might generate a spark including not switching any electrical items on OR OFF.
- ➤ NEVER mix chemicals together unless you are sure that it is safe to do so.
- ➤ Keep out of direct sunlight.

Cyanotype chemicals:

Hydrogen Peroxide
- ➤ Hydrogen peroxide is basically a safe chemical in the strength of solution that we use in cyanotyping. It has oxidising and bleaching properties and is often used as a mild disinfectant and antiseptic.
- ➤ Because it is a clear liquid, care must be taken to ensure that it is not mistaken for drinking water and for this reason alone, do not put it into any container that could be mistaken for a drinking vessel.
- ➤ Store containers in a dark, well ventilated area and remember that pressure may build up in sealed bottles, so be careful to release the pressure slowly when opening them to avoid splashing the liquid around.

Potassium Ferricyanide
- ➤ Despite its name, Potassium Ferricyanide is not as hazardous as it may sound. The crystals or powder must be kept in a tightly lidded container to stop them breaking down and deteriorating. The containers should be kept in a cool place.
- ➤ Potassium Ferricyanide should not be mixed with strong acids as this could cause the release of harmful fumes.
- ➤ Avoid creating dust and don't breath it in or get it in your eyes.

Ferric Ammonium Citrate
This powder is slightly acidic and can cause skin and eye irritation so the usual precautions apply.

Disposal
Disposal of all three of these chemicals, in the quantities that we use, is fairly straightforward: dilute with plenty of water and flush away, ensuring that plenty of water is flushed down the drains afterwards.

The use of ultra-violet light sources
- ➤ Never stare at ultra-violet (UV) light sources as this can damage your eyes.
- ➤ A sensible precaution is to use suitable goggles when working with UV. These can often be obtained from companies that supply them for use with sun beds or for industrial use.
- ➤ Always make sure that any electrical equipment you use is safe by buying it from a reputable company and having it checked over from time to time by an electrician.
- ➤ Be careful to use properly earthed electrical equipment near to wet or damp objects and ensure that water does not splash on to hot lamps, as this may cause them to shatter.

Computer use

➤ Make sure you are sitting comfortably - sitting badly for any length of time can lead to muscle and joint pain. Make sure your lower back is supported, your knees are level with your hips and your feet are flat on the floor. If you are a shortie, like me, you may need a foot rest as your feet probably don't reach the floor!

➤ It's a good idea to get up and walk round for a few minutes periodically so your muscles don't stiffen up.

➤ Your eye height should be just above the top of the screen. The tendancy for people to use portable computers more and more is generating a big group of people with neck and headache problems. If you have a laptop on your lap then your neck is bent at a bad angle with you looking down for long periods. It is much better to plug a standard monitor into your portable computer so it can be placed at a suitable height.

➤ Your forearms should in a straight line with the back of your hand and both should be parallel to the floor. This reduces strain on your wrist and will diminish the risk of developing Repetitive Strain Injury (RSI).

➤ While you are using the mouse your arms should not be extended but should be relaxed with your forearms roughly parallel to the floor and the backs of your hands in line with your forearms. This will reduce stress on your wrists, a common site for RSI. It's also a good idea to learn some keyboard shortcuts to reduce the use of the mouse and therefore strain on your hands and arms. For instance holding the control key down and pressing the p key, usually written as ctrl-P is the equivalent of selecting File > Print.

➤ Try and change the focus of your eyes from time to time by looking into the distance if you can as this will reduce eye strain. Do remember to blink occasionally - the tendancy is to stare at the screen when you are concentrating and especially contact lens wearers may end up with dry, sore eyes.

➤ Oh, and enjoy yourself ....

Using a rotary cutter

Rotary cutters are, to state the blindingly obvious, very sharp, so they need to be used with care.

➤ Keep the guard on when you're not using it. I have one where you squeeze the handle to lift the guard away from the blade. When you release the handle to put it down the guard lifts into place. I like this – one less thing to remember.

➤ Cut away from you not towards you.

➤ Replace the blade frequently – if the blade is blunt you will use more pressure and will be more likely to slip and hurt yourself.

➤ When you are transporting a rotary cutter, lock the guard into place (there's usually a button to do this) and keep it in a case of some sort. Then, if the guard comes off and you reach into your bag for something else, you should retain all your fingers ...

If you are left-handed then the type of rotary cutter I've described above can have the blade on either side of the handle to accommodate right and left-handed users. Carefully unscrew the blade, reverse all the fittings and screw back into place.

Appendix II
- Copyright ...

If you want to use other people's photographs, this includes magazines, newspapers, books etc then make sure you are not breaching anyone's copyright. Note especially that photographs taken of your artwork by someone else are probably copyright to them, even though you own the copyright of the artwork itself.

Your Work

Copyright allows creative people such as artists, photographers, musicians and writers to control the copying and use on-line of their work. Most uses of copyright works require permission from the copyright holder apart from some possible exceptional uses such as private study, teaching in schools or non-commercial research.

I don't think I could do any better than suggest that you consult the www.intellectual-property.gov. uk web site. They have a wealth of information on copyright, written clearly, explaining that copyright protection is automatic as soon as there is a record in any form of what has been created (there is no official registration). However, you may need to prove that you had the work at a particular time and there are ways that you can provide evidence of this. For example, you could deposit a copy with a bank or solicitor. Alternatively, you could send yourself a copy by special delivery post (which gives a clear date stamp on the envelope), leaving the envelope unopened on its return.

It is important to note, that this does not prove that a work is original or created by you. But it may be useful to be able to show that the work was in your possession at a particular date. For example where someone else claims that you have copied something of theirs that was only created at a later date.

Using someone else's work

With current technology it is very easy to copy an image; you just point a digital camera at it or put it on your scanner. However you need to consider whether it is legal or ethical to do so. If you take your own original photograph or produce your own artwork then you can use it in any way you wish as you will hold the copyright. So, if you have one, why not keep a camera with you and photograph anything that interests you. You can store your photographs on your computer or a CD/DVD which will then give you a 'stash' to dip into whenever you want to incorporate a picture into your work.

There is a wide selection of copyright free imagery available in books and on the Internet. Some images are completely free to use, some you can only use for non commercial purposes or for a restricted number of times.

Unless it is stated otherwise assume that books and magazines are copyright and you would, therefore, have to get written permission to use something from them. If you want to use any copyright material you can write to the copyright owner explaining what you want to use and how you want to use it. You can then work out with the owner any terms and conditions and possible payment of a fee or royalty.

Copyright is there to protect your work and other people's. At its basic level it is a 'do as you would be done by' situation. If you wouldn't want anyone else to copy your work without permission don't do the same to anyone else.

The above is only a very brief summary, to the best of my understanding, of a complex subject – if you are in any doubt about your use of a particular image I would strongly recommend that you seek and obtain specific written permission or take informed legal advice.

For artists working outside the UK you will have to check the rules for your particular area. For somewhere to start have a look at http://www.wipo.int/directory/en/ - this page gives a list of many countries with their respective copyright offices. In the USA have a look at www.copyright.gov. If you want to search further on the Internet for information on copyright you may find it under 'Intellectual Property'.

A couple of other web sites you might like to have a look at are:

www.startanartbusiness.co.uk/art-copyright-law-protecting-artwork.html

www.lr.mdx.ac.uk/copyright/index.htm

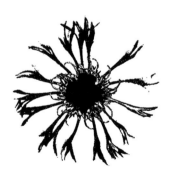

Suppliers ...

There are many good suppliers out there. Here I've only included ones that I know stock the sort of products used in this book. If I've missed anyone good out, please let me know - I may be able to include them on my web site.

Textile Suppliers

(in alphabetical order)

Art van Go

The Studios
1 Stevenage Road
Knebworth
Hertfordshire
SG3 6AN
Tel: 01438 814946
Web site: www.artvango.co.uk
Mail order, shop and the famous travelling van.

Colourcraft (C&A) Ltd

Unit 6
555 Carlisle Street East
Sheffield
S4 8DT
Tel: 0114 242 1431
Web site: www.colourcraftltd.com

Fibrecrafts

George Weil & Sons Ltd
Old Portsmouth Road
Peasmarsh
GUILDFORD
Surrey
GU3 1LZ
Tel: 01483 565800
Web site: www.fibrecrafts.com
Mail order and showroom

Rainbow Silks

Mail Order:
6 Wheelers Yard
High Street
Great Missenden
Bucks
HP16 0AL
UK
Tel: 01494 862111
Shop:
85 High Street
Great Missenden
Buckinghamshire
UK
Tel: 01494 862929
Web site: www.rainbowsilks.co.uk

Rio Designs

Flint Cottage
Treacle Lane
Rushden
Buntingford
Herts.
SG9 0SL:
Tel: 01763 288234
Web site: www.riodesigns.co.uk

Thermofax Screens

Stone Creek Silk (me)

Stone Creek House
Sunk Island
East Yorkshire
HU12 0AP
Tel: 01964 630630
Web site: www.stonecreeksilk.co.uk

Thermofax Screens (Claire Higgott)

Foxley Farm
Foxley
Towcester
NN12 8HP
Web site: www.thermofaxscreens.co.uk

Panenka Design Produkte Munchen

85649 Otterlo
Hauptstr. 7a
Germany
Tel: +49 (0)89 67 73 26
Web site: www.patchworkshop.de
Guenther Panenka, as far as I know, is the only manufacturer of thermofax machines outside the UK. He speaks very good English so you can contact him if you have any queries or would like to order a machine.

Welsh Products Inc

PO Box 6120
Arnold
CA 95223-6120
Tel: 800-745-3255 or 209-795-3285
Web site: www.diyprintsupply.com

PhotoEZ

EZScreenPrint LLC

3640 N Crane Place
Casa Grande
AZ 85122
Tel: 520-423-0409
Web site: www.ezscreenprint.com

Art Threads/Ginny Eckley (USA only)

2423 Kings Forest Drive
Kingwood TX 77339
Tel: 281-358-2951
Web site: www.photoezsilkscreen.com

Transparency Film and Papers

LLoyd Paton

Web site: www.lloydpaton.co.uk/
Source for A3 Acetates for Photocopier/Laser printer/Inkjet

on-line paper co uk

Unit 19 Bassetts Manor
Butcherfield Lane
Hartfield
East Sussex
TN7 4LA
Tel: 01892 771245
Web site: www.on-linepaper.co.uk
Fast, efficient, friendly service and a brilliant range of all things paper.

United States

Dharma Trading Company

P.O. Box 150916
San Rafael
CA 94915
USA
Tel: (800) 542-5227 Toll-free from anywhere in the USA & Canada
Tel: (415) 456-7657 Everywhere else
Web site: www.dharmatrading.com

Dick Blick Art Materials

P.O. Box 1267
Galesburg
IL 61402-1267
USA
Tel: (800) 828-4548
Web site: www.dickblick.com

Bibliography ...

This is a list of books I particularly like or have found useful. You can never have too many books ... !

Direct printing:

Altered Photo Artistry

Turn Everyday Images into Works of Art on Fabric
Beth Wheeler & Lori Marquette
C&t Publishing – 2007
ISBN: 978-1-57120-440-0

Next Steps in Altered Photo Artistry

Beth Wheeler
C&T Publishing - 2009
ISBN: 978-1-57120-658-9

Artistic Photo Quilts

Create Stunning Quilts with your Camera, Computer & Cloth
Charlotte Ziebarth
C&T Publishing - 2009
ISBN: 978-1-57120-600-8

Image Transfer

Quilting your memories

Inspiration for Designing with Image Transfer
Sandy Bonsib
Martingale & Co – 1999
ISBN 1-56477-251-9

Paper & Metal Leaf Lamination

A mixed media approach with cloth
Claire Benn, Jane Dunnewold & Leslie Morgan
Committed to Cloth & Art Cloth Studios - 2008
ISBN: 978-0-9551649-3-4

Digital Negatives & Positives

Cyanotypes on Fabric

A blueprint on how to produce ... Blueprints
Ruth Brown
S C Publications - 2006
ISBN: 978-0-9554647-0-6

Blueprints on Fabric

Innovative uses for cyanotypes
Barbara Hewitt
Interweave Press - 1995
ISBN: 0-934026-91-2
This is the book that started me off with cyanotyping. I understand it's now out of print but you may be able to find a copy.

Cyanotype

the history, science and art of photographic printing in Prussian Blue
Mike Ware
National Museum of Photography, Film and Television - 1999
ISBN: 1-900747-07-3
The definitive and comprehensive guide to the chemistry, history and preservation of cyanotypes.

Blue Prints

The natural world in cyanotype photographs
Zeva Oelbaum
Rizzoli International Publications Inc - 2002
ISBN: 0-8478-2432-2

Transforming Fabric

30 Creative Ways to Paint, Dye and Pattern
Cloth
Carolyn A Dahl
Krause Publications – 2004
ISBN 0-87349-616-7
As the title suggests, this book is cornucopia
of techniques written in Carolyn's highly
individual voice. Only five pages refer to
using Inkodyes but I wanted to include it here
because I like it so much.

Making Digital Negatives with an ink-jet printer

Mike Ware
Version 7 - 2010
ISSN: 2040-8501
(available through Siderotype.com

Making Digital Negatives for Contact Printing

Dan Burkholder

The Inkjet Negative Companion

Dan Burkholder
Digital book available from Dan's website
www.danburkholder.com

Image Manipulation and Digital Art

Photoshop Elements 8 for Windows

the missing manual
Barbara Brundage
O'Reilly - 2009
ISBN: 978-0-596-80347-6
The 'must have' book if you use Photoshop
Elements. There are different books for each
version of the software.

How to Cheat in Photoshop Elements 8

David Asch & Steve Caplin
Focal Press 2010
ISBN: 978-0-240-52187-9

Photoshop Fine Art Cookbook for Digital Photographers

John Beardsworth
Ilex - 2006
ISBN: 978-1-904705-74-1

Photoshop Blending Modes Cookbook for Digital Photographers

John Beardsworth
Ilex - 2005
ISBN: 1-904705-68-5

digital Essentials

the quilt maker's must-have guide to images, files
and more!
Gloria Hansen
The Electric Quilt Company - 2008
ISBN: 1-893824-64-0

Photo Art

Tony Worobiec & Ray Spence
Collins & Brown – 2003
ISBN: 1-84340-055-3
A lovely and inspirational book on art photography
giving many ideas on ways of working and
combining techniques. I particularly liked the
sections on photomontage, multiple-exposure and
photograms.

The Digital Canvas

Jonathan Raimes
Ilex - 2006
ISBN: 978-1-904705-76-6

Digital Photo Artist

Creative Techniques and Ideas for Digital Image-
making
Tony Worobiec & Ray Spence
Collins & Brown - 2005
ISBN: 1-84640-148-7

Digital Art Studio

Techniques for Combining Inkjet Printing with Traditional Art Materials
Karin Schminke, Dorothy Simpson Krause Bonny Pierce Lhotka
Watson Guptill Publications – 2004
ISBN: 0-8230-1342-1

Creative Digital Photography

Michael Busselle
David & Charles - 2002
ISBN: 978-0-7153-2241-3

The Complete Guide to Digital Photography

Michael Freeman
Thames & Hudson - 2006
IISBN: 978-0-500-54325-2

Digital Printing

Epson Complete Guide to Digital Printing

Rob Sheppard
Lark Books - 2008
ISBN: 978-1-60059-263-8

The Digital Printing Handbook

A photographer's guide to creative printing techniques
Argentum - 2002
ISBN: 1-902539-17-X

Mastering Digital Printing

Harald Johnson
Thomson - 2005
ISBN: 1-59200-431-8

Screen printing & print making

Thermofax Printing

Bringing personal imagery alive
Claire Benn & Leslie Morgan
Committed to Cloth - 2010
ISBN: 978-0-9551649-6-5

Solar Plate

Printmaking in the Sun
An Artist's Guide to Making Professional quality Prints using the Solarplate Method
Dan Welden and Pauline Muir
Watson Guptill Publications – 2001
ISBN: 0-8239-4292-8

Index ...

Also by the author:

Cyanotypes on Fabric

Learn how to create these beautiful, subtle, blueprints on gorgeous fabrics.

You'll also find out how to create digital negatives, how to colour your cyanotypes and how to take care of your prints.

Ruth Brown

Stone Creek Silk

Stone Creek House, Sunk Island

East Yorkshire, HU12 0AP, UK

Tel: 01964 630630

Email: ruth@stonecreeksilk.co.uk

Web site: www.stonecreeksilk.co.uk